the ROADMAP
to a RichLife

To your RichLife !

Ben Henderson

the ROADMAP
to a RichLife

Success with Life, Relationships, and Money

BEAU HENDERSON

Published by Sound Wisdom, Shippensburg, Pennsylvania. All rights reserved. This book is protected by the copyright laws of the United States of America. This book may not be copied or reprinted for commercial gain or profit. The use of short quotations or occasional page copying for personal or group study is permitted and encouraged. Permission will be granted upon request.

The reader of this publication assumes responsibility for the use of the information. The author and publisher assume no responsibility or liability whatsoever on the behalf of the reader of this publication. While efforts have been made to verify information contained in this publication, neither the author nor the publisher make any warranties with respect to errors, inaccuracies, or omissions.

All readers are advised to seek competent lawyers and accountants to follow laws and regulations that may apply to specific situations.

For more information on foreign distribution, call 717-530-2122.

Reach us on the Internet: www.soundwisdom.com.

Sound Wisdom
P.O. Box 310
Shippensburg, PA 17257-0310

ISBN 13 TP: 978-0-7684-1101-0
ISBN 13 Ebook: 978-0-7684-1102-7

For Worldwide Distribution, Printed in the U.S.A.
1 2 3 4 5 6 7 8 / 19 18 17 16

CONTENTS

THE RICHLIFE STORY

I f you've been frustrated in the past with your finances, if you have failed when trying to get out of debt, start a business, create a budget, or save for retirement, then this book is designed for you. It turns the problem of money into an exciting puzzle that includes not just your finances, but *all* the pieces important to creating a healthy, wealthy, and fulfilled life with a purpose. This is my definition of a RichLife and it is my mission to help you discover yours.

The question of what makes a person *rich* came to me one day after meeting a highly respected business man, a multi-millionaire we'll call Richard. He was someone who in my eyes had truly made it. Richard had *followed the money* and arrived, achieving success in business and an enviable net worth. I was on the same path myself, and I couldn't wait to meet him and hear what he had to say. I drove up to his sprawling estate, knocked on the door, and met the man who had achieved every single financial goal he ever set for himself.

I was shocked see just where *following the money* had led him.

Richard wasn't old, but he shuffled when he walked, having just recovered from a dangerous and massive heart attack. He led me through his beautiful but cold house, filled with beautiful but inanimate things. I found out in the first fifteen minutes of our conversation that his wife had recently left, his grown kids no longer talked to him, and he had no relationship with his grandchildren. We sat down in his study and we talked. Not once did he smile. He told me his story and he held out his hands. "This is what it comes down to," he said. And I looked at his empty palms and saw that everything of real value to him had been lost.

I left his mansion that night in a daze. It was like finding out that there was no Santa Claus. Everything I had been taught about money simply wasn't true. I drove home thinking about all the people I had met over the years and I realized that what made them happy wasn't just money alone. It was a combination of assets that included life purpose, memorable experiences, and the people they cared most about and loved.

Being rich doesn't just happen. It requires planning and focus, decisions and guiding principles. But what are those guiding principles and what should you be investing in? How do you know when your assets are exposed to too much risk? What can you do to recover from big mistakes or loss, and what should you be focused on when trying to save and reduce debt? The RichLife philosophy is about more than just the money in the bank. It embraces the people, ideas, and values important to you. This book is designed to help you put together not just a sound financial plan, but your own version of a RichLife Plan. It will cover the following:

- The Intersection of money, purpose, and passion

- Getting more of what you want

- Giving more where you want

- Developing a saving habit

- The RichLife formula for dealing with debt

- Investing in your retirement, relationships, and creating memorable experiences

Along the way you'll meet lots of hard-working individuals like you—people who are on their own journey creating their definition of a RichLife—sharing their stories from the road.

Most advisors focus on the investment, but my focus is on *the investor*. Sure, I can help you find the best mutual fund, life insurance product, or asset allocation, but my intention is to help you on your way toward investing *in a fulfilled life*. I want you to be *rich* in every sense of the word. I want you to have great relationships, meaningful work, and money in the bank. This approach to investing has helped thousands of people build what I call a *RichLife*, and it is what this book will help you achieve.

So let's roll up our sleeves and get to work. Your RichLife is out there waiting for you.

BEAU HENDERSON
Founder and CEO, The RichLife Group

Part One

THE RICHLIFE PRINCIPLES

My RichLife started about 11 years ago when my dear friend Terry made me really mad. You see, my grandma got sick and she came to live with us. I didn't know at the time that it would be only for a short period. I was very focused on my career at the bank, on building my part-time business and raising my own family. It irritated me when I would come home from work to find not only my two teenagers, but also my husband, my duties for the home, my business, my customers, and then there's Grandma. She'd be there standing at the door, greeting me and wanting my time. I know that sounds terrible, but it was how I felt.

One night I was talking on the phone to my friend about my frustrations with my business and grandma and her tone of voice changed. She said to me, "Carla, you're not going to like what I'm about to tell you. But I love you as a friend, and only a friend would be honest enough to tell you this: Get over it. Stop worrying about your business and take care of the real business: the business of being a granddaughter to the grandma who gave you her whole life."

And she was right. I got really mad at her. I mean, so mad that I didn't talk to her for a week. But my point is this: I thought long and hard about what my friend told me. To quit focusing on the things that didn't matter, my job and the business, all that stuff is irrelevant when it comes to the people in your life, because that's what makes your life truly rich. A long story short, my grandma was with us for eight months. Those were the best eight months of my life. Grandma shared her RichLife with us. I mean, I heard stories I had never heard my whole adult life! Grandma really opened up and shared the real Grandma with me. In turn, I opened up to her. I told her about my business and what I was hoping to do, and talking to her really helped me figure out what I was all about. I only had her with me for those few months, but I've always carried that time with me in my heart. I thank my friend Terry every day for being a good enough friend to tell me the truth. To tell me to get my priorities straight and take care of things that really matter. And it's funny how when you start with that, the other stuff just falls right into place.

—CARLA GARDINER

Before beginning the actual work of building, the RichLife program begins with a series of questions designed for discovery. When you know *why* you are doing something, the discipline required for the *how* becomes much easier. We will be asking questions such as: *What motivates you? Why do you want to be successful with your business? Why do you want to make X amount of dollars every month?* For most people, the answers to these questions have something to do with the people important in their lives.

"I want to make more money so I can take care of my family," is perhaps the most common response I hear, yet investments in family aren't usually included in the asset allocation of our life. What usually happens is that the people we care about most are the people who end up getting left out when we try to focus on our goals. It's sad but ironic how the very people whom it's all for can often end up being the people we hurt the most.

Following the RichLife principles as you begin building your roadmap to success will help you make sure that nothing important, like talks with Grandma, gets left out along the way. We consider investments in your relationships just as important as the investments you set aside for your retirement savings. We want you to get to achieve your goals and get to where you want to go, but *how* you make the journey is also part of your RichLife.

The following RichLife principles offer you a new way to look at your work, your relationships, and even your finances. These principles are at the heart of the RichLife philosophy and can be applied to every chapter of the book. In other words, all of the RichLife principles are designed to work together, incorporating all aspects of your life to create a roadmap to true wealth. Don't think of it as just another chore, but rather as an exciting journey; because if you're not having fun along the way, then you are missing out on so many more opportunities to *live rich*.

Chapter 1

THE REALITIES OF HARD/EASY

"The beginning is the most
important part of the work."
—PLATO

The principle of Hard/Easy is what I call the master investment. It is a habit that when adopted makes the biggest difference between those who achieve success and those who don't. It can be applied to every area of your life—business, finances, relationships—and is the biggest secret to success that no one is talking about. Who can apply the investment of hard/easy?

- Old or young and young at heart

- Educated or non-educated

- Rich or poor

- Male or female

Did I leave anybody out? Nope. The investment of hard/easy is not exclusive. It applies to *everybody*. Application of Hard/Easy is your call to action. It is the one thing that *you can do* right now regardless of age, income, or job status that will make the greatest difference between changing your life and not changing your life.

PAYING THE PRICE OR PAYING THE COST

Most people when given the choice will do the easy thing first. They reason: if it's going to be hard either now or later, well then I'll pick later! They will deal with it when it happens. After all, they think, why do today what you can put off until tomorrow? Let me put it to you another way.

The "hard" that comes later is not the same as the hard that comes now. When you fail to pay the *price* upfront, the *cost* in the end is huge. For example, if you do the hard thing now of saving one hundred and fifty dollars a month, it will be much easier to retire in 30 years. In 30 years, you still have to find a way to fund your retirement. It will be much harder to come up with a large nest egg when you are age 65 than when you are age 25, tucking away one hundred and fifty dollars a month and capitalizing on the power of compound interest.

We all know the saying, "the rich get richer and the poor get poorer." The principle of hard/easy sheds a great deal of light on why this is true. It also means that if you want to change the direction you are going in, it's going to require more work up front. Things will get easier down the road if you do the hard work now, and if you don't do the hard work now, the hard work later will be worse. The good news here is that if you do the hard part now, it will be a piece of cake down the road.

Hard/easy is a habit of discipline. When the discipline to do the hard thing is consistently applied, a habit is developed. Once that habit becomes a part of your life, a kind of momentum happens and your productivity shifts. The things in your life that once seemed like humongous tasks become manageable, because the hard work behind you starts to pay off in dividends ahead.

Let's look at hard/easy in terms of diet and exercise to understand how this momentum is created. It's very difficult for someone who is out of shape to get into the habit of running two miles a day. Their body is heavier, their muscles weak, and they are not used to the exercise. It requires far more energy for a non-runner to get out there and log in two miles than someone who has been training for the past two years and can easily run a 5K without even losing wind. This is because the more you run, the more weight you lose, the more muscle tone you develop, and the easier running gets. It gets easier physically and easier mentally because you start to feel good, and the better you feel, the more you practice the habit.

The following diagram developed by Steve D'Annunzio, founder of the Soul Purpose Institute, illustrates the momentum created by practicing the discipline of hard/easy.

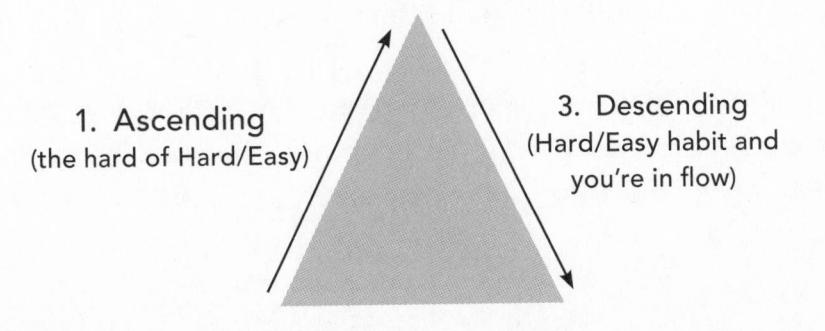

2. Habit Developing
(hard decreases as discipline become
habit and productivity shifts)

1. Ascending
(the hard of Hard/Easy)

3. Descending
(Hard/Easy habit and
you're in flow)

STEPS TO HARD/EASY

- **The Ascending**: Ladies and gentleman, I hate to break it to you, but this part is hard. If you want to get into the discipline of doing something you've never done before, it's going to require a bit of muscle. You need to get up, show up, and keep showing up, even if you don't want to. Keep pushing yourself up that hill by keeping the bigger goal in mind. And don't beat yourself up when you backslide. It's part of the process. Sometimes we even slip and fall. It's okay. Just get back up again and keep going.

- **Habit Developing**: This is where you'll start to see a little light at the end of the tunnel. The weight of the hard will feel a little lighter, and one or two good things will start to arrive, rewarding you for the hard work you've done up to this point.

- **Descending**: You've developed a habit now that has become a part of your ethic. You've gotten more efficient so this habit takes you less time than it did at the beginning, during the hard ascent.

Positive things are happening every week because now, you're in what's called "the flow." Productivity increases, profits increase, and you start to see the fruit of your labors.[1]

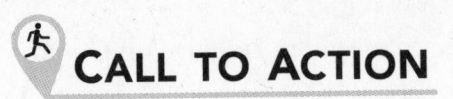 CALL TO ACTION

Step #1: Practicing hard/easy can be done in any area of your life. What area do you want to start with? *Commit to practicing the habit of hard/easy by circling one of the following life areas:*

- Work

- Study or school

- Relationships including trips and adventures

- Finances such as saving or debt reduction

- Business including current and new ventures

- Personal or spiritual growth

- Health and exercise

Step #2: What is stopping you from practicing hard/easy? What are you afraid of? What is the worst case scenario? *Identify the obstacle, release the fear, and create the energy to do the hard.* Write down one obstacle, fear, or worst case scenario related to the task of hard/easy:

- Obstacle: _____

- Fear: _____

- Worst case scenario: _____

the ROADMAP to a RichLife

Step #3: Do the work up front, take action, and give up the procrastination. Set aside a specific period of time or time of day when you will make a conscious effort to focus on the task of hard/easy. For example, you will practice hard/easy in the area of health and exercise by running from 8 to 8:30 Monday through Friday. Identify both the period of time and the day or days of the week so you can hold yourself accountable. Then show up and do what you say you are going to do.

- Day(s) of the Week: _____

- Time of the Day: _____

- I will do the following: _____

  _____

  _____

  _____

  _____

Remember: the practice of hard/easy means it will be hard at first! As your mindset shifts and you begin to develop the habit, you'll find that doing hard becomes your consistent behavior. If you put this book down and never pick it up again, this one habit alone is the most important thing you can do to begin creating the RichLife that you deserve.

ENDNOTE

1. Steven D' Annunzio, founder of the Soul Purpose Institute and author of *The Prosperity Paradigm*.

Bonus Gift: Download your free copy of The RichLife Action Guide at www.RichLifeActionGuide.com.

Chapter 2

WELCOME TO LIFE SCHOOL

"The most important question a person can
ask is, Is the Universe a friendly place?"
–Albert Einstein

Have you ever found yourself in the same bad position over and over again, whether it be the same kind of relationship, the same money problems, the same job issues, or anything else that seems to be attracted to you? You keep hoping that *this time it will be different*, but in the end you keep repeating the same mistakes. Chances are there is a lesson there that has not been learned. This lesson contains exactly what you need to know to move on to the next step of creating what you want. The reason you keep repeating the same mistake isn't because you are an idiot, because someone is out to get you, or because you just have bad luck. The reason you are stuck is because you, along with all the rest of us, are enrolled in a program known as Life School.

The way Life School works is the same way any academic program or curriculum is designed to function. You first have to complete a core curriculum of general studies before you can advance to your major classes. And within the core curriculum there are certain quizzes, tests, and classes that you must pass as prerequisites before you can move forward. An example would be completing Spanish 101 and 102 before you can move on to the Spanish 200 and 300 level classes. If you don't pass a required course you have to take it again until you get the passing grade.

Repeating the same mistakes over and over simply means that, according to Life School, you haven't learned the lesson yet or passed the test.

A mentor and dear friend of mine, Steve D'Annunzio, shared the concept of Life School with me several years ago, and it was this paradigm shift that had the most dramatic effect on the success in my professional and personal life.

HOW DO YOU VIEW THE EXPERIENCE CALLED LIFE?

When it comes to our beliefs, there are those we have chosen and those we have been given. As an adult, sooner or later the time comes to re-evaluate those beliefs. You want to make conscious choices. To ask yourself whether or not a belief is helpful, whether or not it serves you. In this chapter, I offer you a new way of looking at the "bad" things that happen in your life.

When I started viewing life more like a school as opposed to a battlefield filled with potential enemies, my life and success began to improve dramatically. The "bad" things that happened were no longer a punishment but lessons, as it were, designed like a test or a class to lead me to the next "grade level." This has become a very productive way to view failure. When something doesn't go the way I expected or hoped, I am able to look at the experience as a road marker, or a sign, alerting me to areas that need my attention. I stop and ask myself, what is the lesson here? What am I missing? Sometimes, I am directed to a different path altogether. Viewing life in this way, failure is no longer "bad" but friendly. The things we have to go through that are at times unpleasant have the ability to teach us the wisdom we need to move forward. This is how we get unstuck from the patterns that have been holding us back from achieving our goals, dreams, and the RichLife we deserve.

THE LIFE SCHOOL CURRICULUM

If you find yourself stuck in an unhelpful pattern of failure and regret, it just means you haven't learned the lesson yet. Instead of blaming yourself or others for your failure, redirect that energy. Ask yourself, "What is the lesson here?" Look at life as a continuous learning experience much like a college or university.

We each have a specific curriculum to master. Life provides us with the *exact curriculum we need* and the lessons we must master, however painful, in order to move forward and achieve our life purpose. It can seem that some people have an easier time in Life School than others. It's true that each time a lesson is repeated, it gets even more painful. It also seems that the most powerful life purposes come from going through life's most difficult curriculums. Answer the call, and you'll discover the purpose. These are the people who become most valuable to society because of the wisdom they have to offer. This wisdom is often learned through a particularly difficult curriculum at Life School. These people can teach us the most as we go through our own curriculum.

We don't get to choose what will happen. But we always have a choice as to how we are going to respond. By choosing to gain wisdom, we are able to offer a greater gift to the world. How will you choose to view this experience called life?

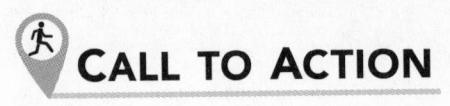 # CALL TO ACTION

Step #1: You can view life as a battlefield, a game, or as a school. You can fight to win, trick and deceive to win, or you can learn to win. Viewing life as a school means there are no failures, only lessons. Print up the following reminder of the Life School curriculum and hang it in a visible place important to you.

---

1. We live in a school I call life.

2. There are no mistakes, only valuable lessons.

3. The lesson is to be repeated until it is learned.

4. Each time a lesson is repeated, it becomes more painful.

5. The greatest lesson to learn is to choose love over fear.

Step #2: Look for the Lessons. Take a moment to think about your most recent or hardest disappointments. The lessons might not be readily apparent. It might take some thinking and it could cause some discomfort. Try to avoid unhelpful attitudes of blame and focus solely on the lesson.

List three things that didn't turn out as you had planned.

1. _____

2. _____

3. _____

What were the lessons that you learned?

1. _____

2. _____

3. _____

What did you have to go through to learn those lessons?

1. _____

2. _____

3. _____

Step #3: Apply the lessons. They are yours. Be aware of them, how they can help you and others to do better next time. Choose one lesson identified in the above steps and continue your discovery with the following questions:

What was the result of learning the lesson?

_____

_____

_____

_____

_____

What do you, or will you, do differently as a direct result of learning this lesson?

_____

_____

_____

_____

_____

Who can you share this lesson with?

_____

_____

_____

_____

_____

Bonus Gift: Download your free copy of The RichLife Action Guide at www.RichLifeActionGuide.com.

Chapter 3

AN ATTITUDE OF GRATITUDE

"Gratitude can transform common days into
thanksgivings, turn routine jobs into joy, and
change ordinary opportunities into blessings."
—WILLIAM ARTHUR WARD

One of the most powerful but under utilized universal laws that governs everyone's life is the Law of Attraction. It basically states that what we think about and focus on most often expands in our life.

If this is true, wouldn't it make sense to focus on the things we want, the people and circumstances that we are grateful for, rather than those we don't like? As the saying goes, it's the squeaky wheel that gets the grease, and as human beings we often get our wheels spinning on a negative track. What if you made the conscious decision to focus on the things you were grateful for instead? What would that feel like? How would the circumstances of your life change?

Even if you are on the fence about the Law of Attraction, a recent study done by Professor Martin E.P. Seligman at the University of Pennsylvania points to the powerful effects of gratitude on our overall mood. The author of the book *Authentic Happiness: Using the New Positive Psychology to Realize Your Potential for Lasting Fulfillment,* Seligman is founder of a new branch of psychology that focuses on what makes us happy rather than what makes us dysfunctional. His research, along with growing studies supported by other scholars in the field, suggests that an attitude of gratitude actually makes us feel better. Gratitude is a key component of inner happiness, well-being, and a sense of self-worth. Perhaps the most talked-about experiment that illustrates this point centers around an assignment Seligman developed for his students while teaching a course on positive psychology.

HOW TO CREATE A GRATITUDE VISIT

The assignment as created by Seligman invites you to create what he calls "gratitude visits." He recommends all readers to do the exercise and gives the following instructions:

1. Select one important person from your past who has made a major positive difference in your life and to whom you have never fully expressed your thanks. (Do not confuse this selection with someone who is a newfound romantic love interest in your life or with someone who is influential and offers the potential of future gain.)

2.   Write a testimonial just long enough to cover one laminated page. Take your time composing this; Seligman's students took several weeks composing their statements, and kept a notebook and pen by their bedside tables so they could jot things down as they came up.

3.   Invite that person to your home or travel to that person's home. It is important you do this face to face, not just in writing or over the telephone. Do not tell the person the purpose of the visit in advance; a simple "I just want to see you" will suffice.

4.   Read your testimonial aloud and slowly to this person, with expression and eye contact.

5.   Allow the other person time for their reactions. It's important not to be in any kind of a hurry. You might find yourselves sharing further memories and stories as you share the concrete details and events that have made this person so important to you.[1]

THE GATEWAY TO OPTIMISM

People who dwell on the good things, on what is right instead of on what is wrong, tend to be happier, more optimistic people. You get to choose what you think about. Being actively aware of your blessings and being actively grateful for them not only makes you feel good, it also helps you to do good. When you are in an attitude of gratitude, you are more clearly focused on what you want instead of on what you don't want. This kind of focus allows you to create more of the things and circumstances you want to have and experience in your RichLife.

One of the fastest ways to get yourself out of a funk is to take a few moments and count your blessings. This might sound trite, but gratitude does several things for us and all of them are good:

- Gratitude reduces negativity.

- Gratitude improves our relationships with people.

- Gratitude helps us create more of what we want.

Being grateful is an effective and powerful tool that can help you get more of the good things you enjoy into your life.

WHAT IF YOU HAVE TOO MANY PROBLEMS?

When the weight of the world is on your shoulders, it can be hard sometimes to find reasons to be grateful. Those reasons are always there, but then again, so are the problems. The key is to learn how to be content with the way things are even as you set about changing them. This piece on contentment is an important component of mapping your RichLife because, like any worthwhile journey, the process takes time. Your problems aren't going to disappear overnight. In fact, as is the way of problems, if you do manage to solve one or two, another problem will likely pop up to take its place. So what do you do about all these problems? As this well-known Buddhist story demonstrates, you solve the 84th problem:

> *A once well-to-do farmer had heard about a wise man who was a wonderful teacher and went to see him, seeking resolution to a set of distressing problems.*

"I'm a landowner," he told the wise man, "and I love to watch my people working in the fields and to see my crops grow. But last summer we had a drought and nearly starved. This summer, we had too much rain and some of my crops did poorly." The wise man listened and nodded compassionately.

"I have a wife too. She's a good woman and a wonderful wife. But sometimes she nags me. To tell the truth, sometimes I grow tired of her." Again, the wise man nodded.

"I have three children. Two are basically good, and I am very proud of them. But sometimes these two refuse to listen to me or pay me the respect I deserve. My oldest son is not so good. He drinks far too much and now he's wandered off. He's been gone a year and I don't know where he is or even if he's alive." The man began to cry and the wise man's face filled with compassion.

The farmer carried on like this for another hour. When he had exhausted himself, he turned to the wise man and said, "Please tell me what to do," fully expecting to receive an answer that would solve all his problems.

"I cannot help you," replied the wise man. "What do you mean?" the farmer retorted.

"Everyone has problems," the wise man replied. "In fact, everyone has eighty-three problems. You may solve one now and then, but another is sure to take its place. Everything is subject to change. Life is impermanent. Everything you have built will return to dust; everyone you love is going to die. You, yourself, are going to die someday. Therein dwells the problem of all problems, and there is nothing you can do about it."

The farmer was chagrined. "What kind of teaching is this? How can it possibly help me?" "Perhaps it will help you with the eighty-fourth problem," answered the wise man. "What is the eighty-fourth problem?" asked the farmer anxiously. "The problem of not wanting any problems," replied the wise man.

As the story illustrates, your problems are always going to be there. You are not alone with your load—everyone has problems. The key to contentment begins with solving the 84th problem. If you can find a way to accept the fact that you will always have an assortment of problems at your door, then you can move past them to see the good that lies beyond. Learning to be content with everything that you have—even the problems—can be like removing a large boulder or obstruction on the inner path to gratitude.

🏃 CALL TO ACTION

The following exercises are designed to help you practice an attitude of gratitude in your daily life. Choose any one of the following gratitude habits and begin applying that habit to your daily life. Make a commitment to practice the habit for a minimum of one week. Notice how you feel, what happens, and what starts showing up in your life.

Starting the Gratitude Habit

We all have things to be thankful for. Take 30 seconds right now and write down three things/people/events/circumstances for which you are grateful today.

1. _____

2. _____

3. _____

Gratitude Habit #1: The Gratitude Meditation

Take 10 minutes every morning to focus positively on people, events, and situations. This will takes the focus off you and your 83 problems and broaden your perspective and horizons. Go through each of the three things you wrote in the space above and focus on the good things about that person, event, or circumstance.

Gratitude Habit #2: The Gratitude Turnaround

Notice yourself complaining. Try to catch yourself in the act. Take a good look at the complaint, and then turn it around. For example, if the complaint is about how your husband didn't wash the dishes, look for something that he *did* do that you appreciated and focus on that.

Gratitude Habit #3: Fake It 'til You Make It

Sometimes it can be hard to focus on gratitude in situations involving difficult people. Remember, the attitude of gratitude is about you, not them. You are not trying to change anybody other than yourself. As with any new habits, these might take time and persistence to integrate into your life.

While you always strive for sincere gratitude, there are difficult situations when the best response is a "thank you" even if you have to bite back what you really want to say. For example, if a co-worker points out that you have made a mistake, and you have all sorts of good reasons why they shouldn't be pointing out said mistake, resist the temptation to fill yourself with defensive argument. Instead, just say something like, "Thanks for pointing that out," and walk away, sending them a silent blessing. You'll find that this practice makes you feel a thousand times better than you would have had you gone the route of a defensive argument.

It's also worth pointing out, however, that an insincere act of gratitude only hurts you, not the other person. Always strive for sincerity.

ENDNOTE

1. Martin E.P. Seligman, *Authentic Happiness: Using the New Positive Psychology to Realize Your Potential for Lasting Fulfillment* (New York: Free Press, 2002), 72-75.

Part Two

THE RICHLIFE PROGRAM

My RichLife started about seven years ago when I was actually homeless, vagabonding across the US, and in an abusive relationship. It was sort of the bottom—if you are familiar with that term—of a long history of really difficult events and circumstances. I was raised in a really abusive home and ended up with a prescription pill addiction in my early twenties. I also ended up with a blessing—my two beautiful daughters. Through a series of events completely out of my control, this person I was in an unfortunate relationship with was arrested. The arrest happened the week after my youngest daughter was born, and I was set free.

I saw an opportunity to take control of my life again. I was in this place of utter chaos, but I always believed that it's not the events in our life that we are in charge of; it's how we respond to those events. I've definitely been through a whole bunch of events that could have ended me, my life, or ended with me in a really bad place.

The first baby step I took was getting really honest. Asking myself, where am I at? It was a pretty painful discovery. I arrived back to my hometown with nothing. I had to humble myself and get a lot of feedback from people who had been successful at crawling out of similar situations because I had a lot at stake. I had two pairs of little eyes watching me.

For the next three or four years, I had to relearn—sort of like a person who has been in an accident—I had to learn how to walk again. I had to learn the basics of life, how to show up every day, how to have a different response. In my case, I had to learn the hard way and go through some of those really earth-shaking events that wake you up and help you grow up. The "why" for me was life or death. I just couldn't limp along any longer. I had to get honest really fast, because I wasn't willing to pass along the chaos that had become life to my little girls.

It's been seven years now and here I have this amazing husband, my two girls, and my son who was just born six months ago. It's an incredible blessing to be in my mid 30s and have everything that money can't buy. All of my biggest investments now are in family.

I have to say that I am literally grateful for all the bad things, for all of the messes of my past, because they have allowed me to discover my mission today: To touch lives. To inspire people. My first bit of advice is always to not give up. It is so easy, when you've had adversity with a "capital A," to not focus on your goals and your dreams. But if you're a late bloomer like me, then it takes a few hard knocks before you get the lesson learned. I always remind myself: Incomplete successes are not failures. Every baby step counts. Even if it feels like we're going back over the same ground again and again, we're still learning! No

*matter the difficulty you are experiencing, life can have
the happy ending that you may have given up on.*
—ELISE ADAMS, CEO and speaker at LeesyAdams.com

The RichLife program begins with a series of questions
designed for discovery. These questions are designed to get to
the root of your motivations. When you know *why* you are doing
something, the discipline required for the *how* becomes much easier. In the case of Elise above, she knew her situation was dire and
the quality of her children's lives was at stake. For most of us, the
why isn't literally life and death, but it can sometimes feel that way
when you are directionless, drifting through the motions of life as
if sleepwalking.

Wouldn't you like to wake up every morning excited about
what the day holds? Imagine being ready to tackle the challenges,
looking forward to the opportunities, and knowing all the while
that you are making a positive difference in someone's life? The
RichLife program is designed to help you figure out why you are
here. Through this program you will learn how best to apply your
skills and particular personality type to embark on career or mission that makes you feel fulfilled.

Bonus Gift: Download your free copy of The RichLife Action
Guide at www.RichLifeActionGuide.com.

Chapter 4

Start with the Why: What's Your Definition of a RichLife?

"If we did all the things we are capable of,
we would literally astound ourselves."
–Thomas Edison

Most people do not take the time to understand *why* they do what they do. If you are one of those people who haven't taken this first step, then you haven't even scratched the surface of the potential locked within you. What motivates you? Why do you want to be successful with your business? Why do you want to make X amount of dollars every month? Try all or one of the following "why" exercises as a way to get in touch with your own mission, because being clear about what you want is critical. *A clear vision leads to motivation, motivation leads to momentum, and from there you can go anywhere.*

THE BIG "WHY" EXERCISE SERIES

The following exercises are designed to dig deep for a better understanding of what motivates you. Choose the exercise that makes the most sense to you or the one that you find the most difficult, or try them all.

The Lottery Exercise

Imagine you just won a $10 million lottery, but there's one catch—*you can't spend it on yourself.* What would you do? Your answers will give you clues to your life mission because you won't be thinking of yourself. You also won't be limiting yourself by self-imposed beliefs about money. Remember, you have $10 million to spend on other people or organizations. Write your answer below.

_____

_____

_____

_____

_____

_____

_____

_____

The Death Sentence

These questions must be answered in 30 seconds or less. Pick up your pen, read through the questions one by one, and answer them knowing this premise: You are terminally ill but will have perfect health during the time you have left. There are no other restrictions. What would you do if—

- You have $10 million and one year to live?

_____

_____

_____

_____

_____

_____

_____

- You have $10 million and six months to live?

_____

_____

_____

_____

_____

_____

_____

_____

_____

_____

- You have $10 million and one month to live?

_____

_____

_____

_____

_____

_____

_____

_____

_____

Now for the follow-up questions:

- Why do we need a death sentence in order to do what's important to us?

_____

_____

_____

_____

_____

_____

_____

_____

_____

_____

The Six-Year-Old Exercise

If you have something of a clue about what you want to do but you haven't uncovered the why, this exercise is for you. Start with the statement, "I want to _____." Fill in the blank with whatever it is you want to do. (I want to make more money, get paid to write my own songs, get my electricians license, start my own agency—you get the idea.) Next, pretend for a moment that you are a six-year-old kid again and ask yourself, "Why?" For each answer that you get, ask yourself why again until you either reach your real reason or you run out of answers. Continue to ask "why?" until there is no further explanation. When you do, your true motivation won't be too far off.

For example:

- I want to get my electrician's license. *Why?*

- I want to make more money. *Why?*

- I want to be able to buy things. *Why?*

- So I feel like I'm taking care of my family. *Why?*

- Because it makes me feel happy and successful. *Why?*

- Because my spouse is more conservative than I am and needs more savings to feel secure.

Ah. So getting your electrician's license is really about feeling secure. It's at this level you'll find your real reasons for working as hard as you do.

The *why* question is a trick question. It's one that has a clear answer but no clear path. It's essentially a paradox, too. The answer to your *why*, at its core, never has anything to do with money. Never. (Yes, really never.) Of course we all need money to live, but once you identify your life's passion and purpose and start acting from a place of true motivation, the money follows.

WHAT'S YOUR LIFE PURPOSE?

There is a reason why you are here. Each of us has been given a unique combination of gifts and talents, interests and desires that no other human being has. When followed, that particular combination has something unique and great to offer the world. The time has come for you to begin astounding yourself. Now you are ready to identify your life purpose.

CALL TO ACTION

Your life purpose is rooted in the gifts and talents that have been endowed to you. One of the most basic ways to learn your life's purpose is to answer this question: "If you could spend your days doing what you love, regardless of whether or not you received monetary compensation, what would you be doing?" The answer to that will most likely reveal valid clues toward what you were put here on this earth to do.

- What lights you up? What do you love to talk about? When you talk about this subject, your energy is up, you talk faster, and you're happy and excited. Fill in the blank: When I _____ time just seems to disappear.

- What is your definition of a RichLife?

_____

_____

_____

_____

_____

_____

_____

_____

_____

_____

- What are the people/activities/circumstances that you want in your RichLife? Example answers are in parenthesis. Please fill in your own answers in the space provided.

RichLife Personal Goals

What I want to do: (Write my book)

_____

_____

_____

_____

_____

Where I want to do it: (Cabin in the mountains)

_____

_____

_____

_____

_____

RichLife Professional Goals:

What I want to do: (Build a successful business to help others)

_____

_____

_____

_____

_____

Where I want to do it: (My hometown)

_____

_____

_____

_____

_____

Relationship Goals

What I want to do: (Get to know my grandkids)

_____

_____

_____

_____

_____

_____

Where I want to do it: (My house)

_____

_____

_____

_____

_____

Any answer is the right answer for you. This is your definition of *living rich*.

Bonus Gift: Download your free copy of The RichLife Action Guide at www.RichLifeActionGuide.com.

Chapter 5

THE WHEN I, THEN I GAME AND THE ART OF TACKING

What is stopping you from
achieving your RichLife?

Y ou have identified what excites you, what you want to do, who you want to do it with, and where you want to do it. What's stopping you? Beware of the "When I, Then I" trap. Don't let it catch you! This trap is a tool designed for procrastination, rationalization, and keeping you stuck in the mud.

ARE YOU PLAYING THE GAME?

There are many areas of life where I see people playing the *when I, then I* game. In many cases, they aren't even aware they are doing it. The *when I, then I* game is often used a lot in conjunction with the word *retirement*. It goes something like this:

- "When I retire, then I can make time for the grandkids."

- "When I retire, then I can spend more time with my spouse."

- "When I retire, then I can finally join that bowling league."

With younger couples, the *when I, then I* game usually goes something like:

- "When I finish remodeling the basement, then I can take my spouse out to dinner."

- "When I'm done with this big job, then I can go out again with my friends."

- "When I get that promotion, then I'll take my kids to that great amusement park."

The problem with this kind of thinking is that it leads to a bankrupt RichLife. Because you are waiting for some future event, you aren't investing in your RichLife *now*. One of the biggest excuses

I hear is not having enough time. The secret to the issue of time is very straightforward: *You make the time now with whatever amount of time you have.*

There is no more waiting allowed. Your RichLife is out there waiting for you to step up. *Waiting for the ideal time, the ideal amount of money, the ideal circumstance is the exact same thing as not doing anything at all.*

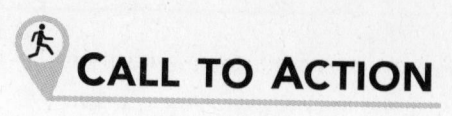

CALL TO ACTION

Write three examples where you are guilty of playing the *when I, then I* game. These examples can come from any area of your life, personal or professional.

1. _____

_____

2. _____

_____

3. _____

_____

Ask yourself:

Where do I play this game most in life?

_____

_____

_____

_____

Why do I play this game? What am I so afraid of?

_____

_____

_____

_____

_____

How can I get out of playing this game?

_____

_____

_____

_____

_____

Break those steps down to a manageable level. Start small. Write down three action steps—things that you can do—that can help you to stop playing the *when I, then I* game and get you moving in the right direction.

What are the action steps needed to move you in the right direction?

1. _____

   _____

2. _____

   _____

3. _____

   _____

THE ART OF TACKING

Your RichLife is not so much a destination to reach but a journey to be on. You can't achieve it all at once, nor would you want to. There are many exciting adventures ahead. The most exciting adventures of all happen when things don't go as we had planned.

A friend of mine likes to compare the way people move through life to boats. He says there are two personality types, the motor boat people and the sail boat people. Motor boat people go from point A to point B in a relatively straight line. If they have a problem, they power through it. They do it the way they've always done it, by revving up the engine. When the engine breaks, they fix it or get a new one.

The sail boat people are on more of a journey. They rely on the wind and their ability to tack, to change the position of the sails so they can effectively harness the breeze. They work with the elements around them in a kind of dance. They are constantly making little adjustments as they go along over the water, and that's the beauty of it. The art of tacking is what they find so exhilarating about the sail.

Tacking is defined as *the act of changing from one position or direction to another.* Sometimes in life, we need to tack, to make an adjustment. Our course of action needs to be altered, just slightly, to optimize attainment of our goal. Sometimes, even our goals change. I invite you to welcome this as part of the journey.

Being flexible is a key component to a RichLife. Seeing and understanding that mistakes are only lessons we haven't learned helps us expand the gray area of our world, because things aren't always black and white. Finding your RichLife is a process that's different for every individual. It's a holistic approach to defining where you want to be by looking at where you have been, where you are now, and where you want to go. If the wind picks up, raise your sails. No wind at all? Roll them up and catch some rays.

Rough seas? Hang in there. We've all been there, and chances are, we'll be there again in the future.

Bonus Gift: Download your free copy of The RichLife Action Guide at www.RichLifeActionGuide.com.

Chapter 6

THE DISC PERSONALITY PROFILE: HOW TO WORK WITH WHO YOU ARE

"Knowing others is wisdom, knowing
yourself is enlightening."
—LAO TZU

The human personality is very complex. Just think about it for a moment—do you know what you will do next? Do you know what your parents, your spouse, your kids, or your best friend will do next? Of course not, but you do have an idea of what they *may* do in certain situations. You have learned to figure them out a little. Whether aware of it or not, you've developed a model or a system in your own head and heart that tells you what to expect from them. This system is a valuable key to developing an understanding of oneself. The challenge is to have a system or model by which to look within so you can better understand how you affect and interact with others.

THE DISC PERSONALITY SYSTEM

In 1928, William Moulton Marston wrote a book called *Emotions of Normal People* in which he popularized the concept of four different primary types of behaviors. We call this the D—I—S—C system: **D**ominant, **I**nfluencer, **S**teadiness, and **C**ompliant. Though a brilliant and diversely creative man credited with developing the first functional lie detector polygraph and inventing the character Wonder Woman, he was a terrible businessman. Marston never protected his intellectual property of the DISC, so there are over 20 different organizations (and counting!) that have used or copied his idea. For the purposes of this book, we will use what we believe to be the most accessible and objective model. What follows is a broad description of the four basic DISC personality types:

- **Dominants** at their most intense are very competitive, driven, direct, and demanding. They are known for being confrontational and results oriented, and they thrive in conditions of change. Think of Donald Trump and the *"You're fired!"* phrase he made famous in his television show, *The Apprentice.* Dominants love a challenge and frequently become very determined when attaining a goal. You typically know where you stand with a D, but here's a tip—they respect you more if you challenge them back. Watch out for them micromanaging if you aren't progressing on a task quickly enough. You won't find much patience here.

- **Influencers** are optimistic and personable. They like to (and do!) talk a lot, are trusting, interactive, and (at times) impulsive. They especially love to talk with others. For them, a stranger is simply someone they haven't had the opportunity to befriend yet. (In other words, they haven't had the chance to influence them yet.) When they do, they will succeed in winning them over to their side. Oprah Winfrey is the classical I. Her interactive and comforting skills, optimism, and energy all conspire to help others feel comfortable in her company. Her trusting nature gets people to open up and bare their souls.

- **Steadiness** people bring calm and stability to most any situation. They are known for their predictability and patience, and they have a gift for accommodating others during conflict, as their presence is just plain soothing. They are great listeners, and for this reason they really connect with people. Though quiet and shy initially, they network by bringing calm to the storm. S types are also excellent at understanding human nature. Some of you may remember Mr. Rogers of the *Mr. Rogers' Neighborhood* television show. Every weekday, he walked into our lives via television, and the first thing he did was to welcome us to "his" neighborhood. He then took off his sweater and hung it up on a hanger (of course) and made us feel right at home. People who exhibit an intense S behavior style are exceptional at doing this. In the hectic world we all live, the S helps us deal with stress and makes us feel that someone really cares.

- **The Conscientious** or C style focuses most on detail and quality. They tend to be skeptical, cynical, and pessimistic. They thrive on data and information, demand accuracy, and have high expectations of others as well as themselves. They are very task oriented and have to work hard to feel comfortable with others. Einstein, Mr. Spock of *Star Trek* fame, and Sheldon on the *Big Bang Theory* TV show are classical, very intense C styles. They feel most comfortable with the specifics and details, and least comfortable with the human aspect of things.

CALL TO ACTION

There are no "best" personality types. Each have positive and negative qualities. It's important to learn how to recognize the wholeness of what makes us who we are. Identify it. Cherish it. Learn its advantages and its limitations. You might as well take advantage of it, because that's what makes us each who we are. In other words, learn how to live with you! *We will all be more successful if we become more comfortable with ourselves.*

Step One: Identify your main personality type. Read over the brief descriptions and circle the type you feel generally best reflects you. If you have a combination of more than one type, be specific about that. If you need more information before you can answer this question, then you are probably a type C. ☺

Dominant   Influencer

Steady   Conscientious

Step Two: Identify your strengths.

1. _____

2. _____

3. _____

Step Three: Identify your weaknesses.

1. _____

2. _____

3. _____

Step Four: Identify the personality type of someone close to you. Think about a conflict you have recently had. Now that you have gained insight into their personality type, how could you have handled the conflict better?

_____

_____

_____

_____

_____

_____

_____

_____

_____

Step Five: Now that you know yourself better, identify a conflict you had recently where you weren't happy with the outcome. With this increased understanding of your strengths and weaknesses, what could you have done to better work with those attributes and positively influence the outcome?

_____

_____

_____

_____

_____

_____

_____

_____

_____

_____

_____

Bonus Gift: Download your free copy of The RichLife Action Guide at www.RichLifeActionGuide.com.

Chapter 7

INVESTING IN HUMAN ASSETS: RELATIONSHIPS AND MEMORABLE EXPERIENCES

George Bernard Shaw wrote a letter to his
friend, Winston Churchill:
*"I am enclosing two tickets to the first night of
my new play. Bring a friend—if you have one."*
To which Churchill responded,
*"Cannot possibly attend first night, will
attend second—if there is one."*

There's nothing like a good friend to make us smile, and nothing like a familiar shoulder to cry on. When was the last time you made an investment to your relationship accounts? Often we spend more time at work than with our family and friends because we have convinced ourselves that the goal of accumulating money is more important. The *business first* mentality or *the end justifies the means* almost always results in an erosion of our most important personal relationships. It also puts the things we love to do—experiences such as attending plays or even performing in them—on the back burner for a later date that may never arrive. These habits do nothing to build the RichLife we deserve.

YOUR LIVING ASSETS

Our assets can be divided into the following three class types:

- **Physical Assets**—this is our "stuff." Our homes, our car, and the diamond ring we inherited from Grandma.

- **Financial Assets**—this is our money, what most people talk about when they do their financial planning. Planning for your RichLife does include a discussion about your financial assets, but that discussion comes *after* we talk about the people in your life, because without these loved ones, what's it all for?

- **Human Assets**—the asset class most easily forgotten—these are the people important to us. Our parents, our spouse, our kids, and our closest friends. This asset class might also include mentors or teachers. It can also include other "live" assets such as four-legged friends, plants, or even fish.

No amount of money can create or replace the human connection and the experience of creating memories together. Playing the *when I, then I* game in this area of our lives is particularly risky and usually leads to bankrupt relationship accounts. It's easy to forget that relationship withdrawals can add up, too. How many times can someone be told, "Not now, honey, later," before they realize that later never comes? Families are the people we count on every day, but if these relationships aren't replenished with regular deposits of time and affection, they can become taxed, over-drawn, and maxed-out. Wait too long and you might find these accounts closed for good.

On a more somber note, we can't get time or people back once they are gone. We all meet our maker in the end. When that time comes and they are gone, they are gone.

CREATING MEMORABLE EXPERIENCES

One of the most important lessons my clients have taught me is that regrets come *not* from the things that we try, but from the things we don't try. Experience is the juice of life. It's why we are here and what really adds to a person's wealth beyond the ordinary parameters of paper assets. The memorable experiences we create now have the power to become the valuable assets we cherish as our memories during our retirement years.

Memories cannot be taxed, stolen, or lost due to a stock market downturn, nor do they depreciate over time. In fact, the more they are visited and revisited, the better they get. There is no penalty, withdrawals can be made as early as the next day, and doing so only makes them stronger. What other asset can boast this kind of return? Creating memorable experiences with the people most important to us is like getting a double return on a single investment. There is no better way to build your RichLife than by making investments of time to create memorable experiences with the people you love.

CALL TO ACTION

How important are relationships to you? Answer the question: If you had great health and enjoyed all the normal physical capabilities, and yet you knew you had exactly six months to live—what would you do?

_____

_____

_____

_____

_____

_____

_____

_____

_____

_____

_____

_____

_____

_____

_____

_____

Was "get a promotion at work" one of your answers? Probably not. I've never had anyone once write down that they would immediately go out and buy a bigger house. Or invest in more stocks. Or ask for a promotion at work. When faced with a short-term ultimatum, most people want to spend time investing in relationships, not things. Let's get to work building a plan that can help you achieve just that.

List your top five relationships:

_____

_____

_____

_____

_____

Investing in Relationships

Set aside a time and day for your relationship investments just as you would your business appointments. Your investment of time doesn't have to be large to be meaningful. Use whatever time you have available to you now, even if it's only five or ten minutes, and communicate the message, *you are important to me.*

Choose one person from the list above. Commit to a five- to ten-minute relationship investment with them.

- What will you do?

- Who will you do it with?

- On what day will you do this?

- During what time frame?

Upgrade Your Flock

The saying goes, "Birds of a feather flock together." Who are the people you are spending time with? Are you learning from them? Are their values in line with yours? Do they add to your RichLife? If the answer to any one of these questions is no, it might be time to limit the time you spend with them in order to make time for other relationships. Fill in the blanks provided with the names of one or more persons:

- I feel energized after spending time with _____

  _____

- I feel drained and exhausted after spending time with _____

  _____

The next time you have an opportunity to spend time with the people listed on the first line, say yes! The next time you are invited to spend time with the people on the second line, politely say no. Remember: "No" isn't a no to someone, it's a "yes" to your RichLife.

Creating Memorable Experiences

Start with something small. I have a client who took his family camping every summer right in their own backyard. When the day finally came that they could afford a real trip to the Grand Canyon, the family was so close and had created so many wonderful memories together; their trip was even more magnificent.

- Pick a person who had a positive influence in your life growing up.

_____

_____

_____

_____

_____

_____

- List your favorite memory of that person or experience.

_____

_____

_____

_____

_____

- Pick an experience that positively influenced or shaped your life.

_____

_____

_____

_____

_____

_____

RichLife Bucket List

Memories rarely just happen. You need to carve out the time to make them happen. Whether you are planning for a family reunion or a trip to Egyptian pyramids, ask yourself, "What memorable experiences do I want to create?"

List three things you want to do:

_____

_____

_____

_____

_____

List three places that you want to see:

_____

_____

_____

_____

_____

_____

List three experiences you want to create with loved ones. (The *key* to creating memorable experiences is to begin by doing small things while planning for the *big* things.)

_____

_____

_____

_____

_____

_____

List three small memorable experiences you can plan for this month:

_____

_____

_____

_____

_____

_____

List three big memorable experiences you can plan for in the next one to five years

_____

_____

_____

_____

_____

_____

How will you begin planning for these experiences? We are going to cover that in the next chapter using the SMART system for setting goals. This system works for all your goals, including your relationships goals and your plans for creating memorable experiences.

Bonus Gift: Download your free copy of The RichLife Action Guide at www.RichLifeActionGuide.com.

Chapter 8

Closing the Gap: The SMART Goal System

"If you don't know where you're going,
any road will get you there."
—Lewis Carroll, adapted from *Alice's
Adventures in Wonderland*

In chapter six of *Alice's Adventures in Wonderland*, Alice asks the Cheshire Cat for directions. She asks him to tell her, "Please, which way should I go from here?" And the cat in his wisdom replies, "That depends a good deal on where you want to get to." When Alice admits that she doesn't much care where she goes, then the cat concludes that it doesn't really matter which way she goes.

Planning for and building your RichLife can be approached in one of two ways—you can either have a plan or leave things up to chance. If you realize like Alice eventually did that you *do* have somewhere in mind you'd like to go, then you will need a plan that has built into it a SMART system for setting goals. The SMART system is an acronym that stands for the following:

- **S: specific**. A goal must be specific in order to be measured. The goal, "I want to make more money," is not specific. The goal, "I want to make six hundred dollars a week," is specific.

- **M: measurable**. You need to have a way of knowing whether or not you have achieved the goal. "I will write every day," is not measurable. Ask yourself, how much will I write? Think of a way you can quantify this. "I will write 1,000 words a day," is measurable.

- **A: attainable**. The goal has to be something that you can actually do. "I will become the first female astronaut in space," is not attainable because it's already been done.

- **R: realistic**. You want to be enjoying yourself, not killing yourself. Make sure your goal is something that *you* can achieve. "I will run seven miles a day," is not a realistic goal for someone who has never run a mile in their life. Start out small. "I will run for ten minutes every morning, Monday through

Friday, between 7:00 and 7:30 am." (Notice the specific and measurable aspect.)

- **T: time sensitive**. Your goal has to have a deadline. Put the pressure *on*. "I will lose thirty pounds," is specific, but there's no deadline. Look at the calendar and do the math. "I will weigh 185 pounds on the evening I turn 55 years old."

If you can't measure a goal, then you can't manage a goal. This is what makes the difference between people who set goals and people who achieve them. State your intention, give yourself a deadline, and map out the steps in a realistic, measurable fashion and you will be well on your way to building your RichLife.

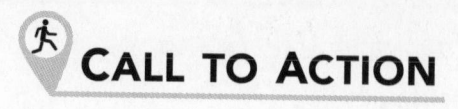

CALL TO ACTION

Your RichLife is composed of six main areas. To help you get clarity in each of these areas, choose one area to focus on now and walk yourself through the SMART goal system.

Draw a circle around one of the following six RichLife areas that you would like to focus on right now in order to achieve clarity of purpose:

Relationships

Personal   **Business**

Health   **Spiritual**

Money

S: Specific. What specifically do you want to do?

_____

_____

_____

_____

_____

M: Measurable. List days, times, word count, number of pounds, or length of activity.

_____

_____

_____

_____

_____

_____

A: Attainable. Can you attain this goal? Why?

_____

_____

_____

_____

_____

R: Realistic. Is your goal realistic? Name the qualifications you have that make this a realistic goal. If you are realizing you need to adjust your goal, do that now.

_____

_____

_____

_____

_____

T: Time sensitive. Write down the exact date—day of the week, month, and year—that you will accomplish this goal.

_____

_____

_____

_____

_____

_____

Bonus Gift: Download your free copy of The RichLife Action Guide at www.RichLifeActionGuide.com.

Chapter 9

CONTRIBUTION

"Do unto others as you would
have them do unto you."
—The Golden Rule

While money alone can't buy you happiness, it just might be true that *giving* away money can. In a 2014 CNN opinion article, Paul J. Zak describes how giving to others releases what he calls the happiness molecule. As the founding Director of the Center for Neuroeconomics Studies and Professor of Economics, Psychology, and Management at Claremont Graduate University, Paul is the author of *The Moral Molecule: The Source of Love and Prosperity*. He contends that our brains are actually wired to promote the giving habit. When we consider others and act in generous ways, our brains reward us by releasing a chemical called oxytocin that actually makes us feel happy. In his studies, Paul found that people who give more—give of their time, money, or of themselves—tend to have happier, fuller lives and better relationships of all types.

Those who ascribe to the holistic idea of a RichLife are already aware of the difference between consuming and contributing, and they actively seek ways to give back to others. This goes back to that attitude of gratitude and how we can pave the way for more riches in our life. Giving back is yet another way to show gratitude, and it can take many different forms:

- The mother who makes room in her busy schedule for one-on-one time with each of her children.

- The businessman who washes the dishes for his wife.

- The professional who donates a half hour every week to read to children at an elementary school.

Even offering a hug instead of a handshake can release more oxytocin—the happiness molecule—making us feel better and more connected to others. Whether you give of yourself, your money, or your time, contribution is one of the tenets of living rich.

SETTING ASIDE THE SEED

Contribution is a word not heard much in today's consumer society. It is an old word that points toward a holistic approach to living in the world. It goes hand in hand with the tradition of setting aside the seed for the future crops of tomorrow in order to ensure that there will be something down the road for us to live on. Our forebears lived by the cycles of the seasons. There were seasons of planting, seasons of harvest, and seasons of rest. Another aspect of this life vital to their well-being was the setting aside of seed.

A part of every harvest—be it potatoes, corn, or wheat—was set aside as "seed grain" for planting the following year. The seed potatoes would not be eaten; neither would the seed corn or wheat. It would be a foolish farmer indeed who ate his own seed. Without that, there would be no future crop.

Even those of us who aren't farmers can understand the cycle of sowing and reaping—what you put into the ground and tend is what will grow. What is neglected will in turn wither and perish. By the same token, care must be taken with regard to how we treat our harvest. A portion of every crop must be set aside and not consumed. Using this as an analogy for our RichLife, it is essential that a portion of all we receive—be it money, goods, or services—be designated as the "seed" for our future tomorrows. This is what we put back out into our community in the form of individual gifts or acts of service to others. The practice of giving ensures the continual flow of riches into our own future lives.

The rules of giving are as follows:

- Giving must be done with no expectation of return.

- You cannot lose what you give away.

- What you put out into the world will then come back to you.

The beautiful thing about giving back is that it has a tendency to multiply in unexpected ways. That's what seeds do—they grow, flower, scatter, and multiply. No one can live a full RichLife without including *contribution* into the equation.

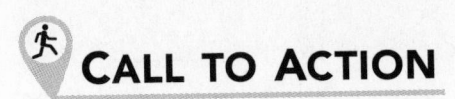 # CALL TO ACTION

Beef up Your Giving Plan

List three ways you can increase your giving this year. For example, you might already be giving money to a local charity. Can you give ten dollars more? Fifty dollars more? Or 100 dollars? Perhaps you volunteer at your local soup kitchen. Can you add another holiday shift to your schedule? Can you coach your son's football team? Can you bring a gift during teacher appreciation day?

1. _____

_____

2. _____

_____

3. _____

_____

How will these contributions improve the lives of others?

1. _____

_____

2. _____

_____

3. _____

_____

Who can you invite to participate in this giving plan with you? Ask a friend to join you or bring a child to help serve in the soup kitchen.

1. _____

   _____

2. _____

   _____

3. _____

   _____

Bonus Gift: Download your free copy of The RichLife Action Guide at www.RichLifeActionGuide.com.

Part Three

SUCCESS WITH MONEY

None of us know how much time we have left on earth. I saw this first-hand at the age of 23 when my father passed away unexpectedly. While he had worked diligently to provide for his family and grow a successful nursery business, he never made plans for what life would be like without him. Losing someone you love is always hard, but when you combine that with the stress of losing income and not having enough money, the situation becomes dire.

No one likes to think about dying. Because of this, many families are caught short when premature death does occur. This subject takes on a very personal note with me because my dad worked very hard and had every intention of taking care of his family. None of us ever imagined he would die at such an early age, including him. We simply weren't prepared.

There are Five Thieves that can sneak up on you and undermine your plans for a RichLife. These thieves can sneak slowly, stealing your savings through the erosive factor of taxes, or they can come in the night and take everything all at once, such as through market loss, chronic illness, or sudden death. When you think of it this way, it only makes sense to put a security system in place. This is at the heart of the RichLife foundation, and we will devote an entire chapter to this subject.

Before you begin investing in financial products, you have to take care of the people and things important to you. Starting with a strong foundation creates a base on which you build. This base begins with an emergency fund, a debt management plan, and protection for the people you love. Without this solid foundation in place, your investments are vulnerable and exposed to risk, much like blocks stacked on top of a wobbly base.

I am now a financial planner in the business of helping people plan for their future. Most of my clients come to me with their concerns for money. I help them see the bigger picture. I teach the average investor how to reach financial independence. My goal is to help them build what I call a RichLife foundation.

—BEAU HENDERSON, founder and CEO
 of RichLife Advisors

A lot of financial professionals approach investing by starting in the middle of the pyramid. They will sell you stocks and mutual funds without asking about you first—your life, your goals, and the people important to you. Even without the help of a professional, most people also tend to start their financial planning in the middle of the pyramid—they invest in their 401(k) at work or start an IRA or, like my dad, they invest everything they have in their business without taking care of their foundation first. This last section of the book focuses on the construction of your financial pyramid. We will start at the base, with your foundation. Success with money begins by addressing the following areas:

- Income planning

- Establishing an emergency fund

- Getting out of the credit card trap

- Debt management

- Protection against the Five Thieves

- Your RichLife commitments

Once we have the foundation in place, we can then start the second phase, which is the accumulation phase. This is when the power of time and compound interest allows your investments to grow. When you get to the top of the pyramid, you enter into what is known as the distribution phase, also known as retirement.

Chapter 10

KNOW YOUR NUMBERS

"If you fail to plan, you are planning to fail."
—BENJAMIN FRANKLIN

Less than five percent of all the people who visit my office know their numbers when they first come in to see me. They might have a little money tucked away in savings; others have done a little investing in mutual funds or real estate. Some people live on a fixed income and receive regular paychecks, while others work on a per project basis, receiving sales commissions. But none of the numbers are concrete. The income and expenses for each month are unknown. *For the most part, people are just hoping that everything works out all right.* This strategy—if you can call it that—is as follows: "I've done a little here and a little there and I work hard. *I hope* when I get to the time of financial need at some point in the future, it will all just work out."

When it comes to prosperity, hoping doesn't cut it. It sets up the conditions of wanting something that isn't there, and these conditions are then perpetuated through simple avoidance or ignorance. Hoping puts someone else in charge. Knowing puts you in the driver's seat. Even if you have no gift for numbers, there is no reason why you can't take charge of your finances today.

What are your *top* three money goals right now?

1. _____

   _____

2. _____

   _____

3. _____

   _____

YOUR FINANCIAL SNAPSHOT

The first step to understanding your current cash flow situation is to work on two important financial statements—your *balance sheet* and your *income statement*. The *balance sheet* will give you a snapshot in time, so to speak, showing you where you stand with regard to assets and liabilities. This is essentially your net worth. Your *income statement* shows you the cash flow, or what is coming in and going out in any given month. It's important when you create your income statement that you are as accurate as possible. Round up, not down. You want your budget to be realistic so that you are successful and not defeated.

Step #1: Create Your Income Statement (what's coming in and what's going out)

1. Get out all your financial statements including your credit card statements, phone bills, and banking account statements or checkbook.

2. Make a list of your income. This is the amount of money *coming in* every month. Write down the amount and the source.

3. Make a list of your expenses. This is the amount of money *going out* every month. Look at your credit card statements as well as your paper receipts. Include expenses such as fuel for both your car and yourself, and any monthly bills for things such as your phone and Internet, car, and health insurance. Also include a category for repairs and maintenance. Factor in an amount that will cover regular oil changes and other maintenance procedures including new tires. Create yet another miscellaneous category to include unexpected expenses such as celebrations and gifts.

Step #2: Know Your Numbers

1. Tally up all the numbers, and take a look at the totals.

2. How much is coming in each month?

3. How much is going out?

4. What is the difference between the two numbers?

Step #3: Create Your Balance Sheet (what you owe and what you own)

1. **A** is for assets. Assets are those items that you own which have a calculated worth in dollars. They include real estate, cars, and savings and investment accounts. Look up the blue book value for your vehicles, identify the current market value of your home, and figure a value for all of your assets if they were sold today.

2. Liabilities include financial obligations that you owe. This includes mortgage debt, student loans, vehicle loans, personal loans and credit card debt. Assets will often have offsetting liabilities such as a house with a mortgage. The house would be an asset and the mortgage would be a liability. If the house value exceeds the mortgage amount, then it creates equity. The increase in equity would in effect increase overall net worth.

3. Calculate your net worth. The difference between what you own and what you owe is your net worth. This is a financial snapshot of where you are in time. Your net worth will change over longer periods of time as the value of what you own increases or decreases, depending on the market, and more of the loan is paid off, decreasing your liability. The balance sheet will help give you an accurate picture of where you stand with regard to *what you own and what you owe* using two categories:

    *   Assets—things that you own that have value.

- Liabilities—obligations that you owe.

Over time, the balance between what you owe and what you own will shift as you make payments. You will own more of the property as you pay off the principal of the loan, decreasing your liability while increasing your assets.

A snapshot of your current net worth is a valuable tool to measure progress and make sure you are heading in the right direction toward your financial goals.

Get financial statement templates and other tools for creating a successful relationship with money at www.RichLifeActionGuide.com.

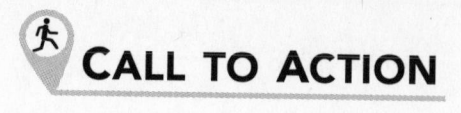

CALL TO ACTION

Now that you know your numbers, your goal is to either increase revenue or decrease liabilities or both. Turn this into a game and make it fun. The *hard/easy* of creating a budget and sticking to it will be a game changer for you and your family.

Play the "Beat the Budget" Game

This is one way to decrease your liabilities. It can be fun because there are two kinds of expenses:

- Those that are set in stone and cannot be changed (example: the monthly rent or mortgage)Those that can be changed by you (example: the amount you spend eating out or going to the movies)Now I'm not saying you should never go out and enjoy yourself. I am suggesting that if you look closely at those expenses *you can control*, you might find opportunities to *beat your budget!* Start small.

- Can you find an extra $1 per day?

- Can you find an extra $10 per week?

- Can you find an extra $25 per month?

- Do you blow $5 per day?

If you can find just five bucks a day then you can begin saving to be a millionaire in 40 years.

5-10-40-1 Plan

- Save $5 a day for 30 days = $150 a month.

- Save for 40 years at a 10 percent average return without touching the principal.

- After 40 years, you will have saved over $1,000,000!

Bonus Gift: Download your free copy of The RichLife Action Guide at www.RichLifeActionGuide.com.

Chapter 11

HOW REAL PEOPLE SAVE MONEY

"Pay yourself first."

I always tell people, "You have to be real to be rich." This means taking an honest look at where you are right now with regard to your finances. For a lot of people, this is the hardest part. Who wants to admit to failure? We all know we should be saving—saving for retirement, college tuition, or just saving for a rainy day—but then life happens and saving goes out the window. There is always something that comes up. This chapter will show you how to save—for retirement, for life, for fun—even in the face of all your 83 problems.

THE CREDIT CARD EMERGENCY TRAP AND HOW TO SOLVE IT

Let's get real about our money problems. One of the most common obstacles to saving that I see is what I call *the credit card emergency trap*. It goes like this.The car gets towed and needs new brakes, the washing machine goes out, and the kid gets sick. You don't have the money to pay for it, but you have a credit card and it's an emergency. After all, that's what credit cards are for, right? So you charge it. The next month instead of taking that two hundred dollars and putting it in your savings account, you put it toward the credit card. You are trying to pay off that big emergency charge and so you stop saving. A few months down the road, another emergency comes up, usually before you have the first emergency entirely paid off, and another charge is put on the credit card. People get stuck in this cycle for years.

There will always be expenses that come up that simply aren't in the budget. Life happens! There is only one way to get out of the credit card emergency trap—you have to create an emergency fund.

What's the Secret Formula?

We all need a cushion. *Having just one month's worth of expenses set aside in an emergency account can prevent 90 percent of all budget-busting emergencies.* When there is no emergency fund in place, the surprise cost goes on the credit card and there it sits, costing you interest every month.

BASE LEVEL SAVINGS FORMULA

For most people, getting out of the emergency credit card trap can be accomplished in three easy steps:

- **Step One:** Create an emergency fund. The first priority of any savings plan should be to have one month of living expenses available for use as an emergency fund. Use the monthly expense number calculated on your income statement. Having this amount in an account you can easily access will keep you out of the credit card emergency fund trap. Open a savings account, money market account, or other savings vehicle that you can easily access during an emergency.

- **Step Two:** Find the extra money to start your emergency savings by making only the minimum payments on your credit cards. Put the rest into your emergency savings account. Do this until you have accumulated one month's worth of living expenses in your emergency fund.

- **Step Three:** Treat your savings plan just like you would any other monthly expense or bill. To increase your chances of success, put it on auto-pilot—have the amount automatically deducted from your checking account or your paycheck.

PHASE TWO: HAMMER THE DEBT

Once you have one month's expenses in place, do the following:

- **Step One:** Hammer debt. Use the formula developed in Chapter 11, *How to Hammer Credit Card Debt*, and keep going until the lowest balance credit card is paid off.

- **Step Two**: Once the first credit card is paid off, reward yourself.

- **Step Three**: Start on the next credit card.

PHASE THREE: CREATE A RICHLIFE FORMULA

Once you have set up your emergency fund and eliminated your credit card debt, it's time to start looking at the big picture of your financial future. It's time to bump up your emergency fund to three months of expenses, and then six months to cover extreme situations such as accidents, illness, or job loss.

- **Step One**: List your top two savings goals. One of your goals can be something fun or personal to you, such as funding a trip or business enterprise. (Example: saving for retirement and saving for a ski trip to Jackson Hole.)

- **Step Two**: Invest 50 percent of your discretionary funds into your emergency fund, and 50 percent into one of your savings goals. For example, if one of your goals is to save for retirement, and you have $400 a month to go toward savings, put $200 in your IRA (or other retirement savings vehicle) and $200 into your emergency fund.

- **Step Three**: Take advantage of free money. Many companies offer their employees a 401(k) plan that pays matching contributions. Even if the match is only a percentage of your contribution, it's free money adding up on your asset column. Why wouldn't you take advantage of it?

SHOW ME THE MONEY FUNNEL

If you are having a hard time coming up with the money to fund your savings account, try giving your expenses a whirl in the money funnel.

The money funnel is a comprehensive list of your expenses. When working with a financial professional, they have tools, programs, and analysis reports they can run for you to help streamline your expenses. The funnel is a program that looks for areas of inefficiency—such as opportunities to refinance a mortgage, lower rates on home or automobile insurance—and identify areas of discretionary expenses such as excessive dining out.

The funnel system:

- Gets better results with the money you are already spending

- Doesn't cost any money to perform (most of the time)

- Uses your existing financial products to squeeze out dollars to fund other programs.

When we take a look at your current investments, policies, and products and run the expenses through the funnel, we are almost always able to free up money. The average funnel finds an additional $200 to $300 dollars that can be moved and applied to your first priority savings. Imagine having an extra $200 to $300 to apply toward reducing your debt, investing in retirement, or putting into your travel bucket for the RichLife you are creating.

INVESTING FOR RETIREMENT

Whenever the subject of retirement savings comes up I often hear the question, "But what about my children's college education?" This is a good question, and I have a good answer: *You can't finance a retirement.* You *can* finance a college education. For this reason, saving for retirement has to be your top priority. Retirement first, and then once the debt is paid off and three to six months of emergency funds are established, we can start filling up the other buckets.

Saving for retirement now means that you will have time on your side. Albert Einstein called the power of compound interest the eighth wonder of the world. Compound interest is the ability of an asset to generate earnings, which are then reinvested in order to generate their own earnings. You can use this eighth wonder to your advantage by applying the Rule of 72: Divide the interest rate into 72 to get the number of years it will take for your savings to double.

4%	Doubles every 18 years	8%	Doubles every 9 years	12%	Double every 6 years
29 years	$5,000	29 years	$5,000	29 years	$5,000
47 years	$10,000	38 years	$10,000	35 years	$10,000
65 years	$20,000	47 years	$20,000	41 years	$20,000
		56 years	$40,000	47 years	$40,000
		65 years	$80,000	53 years	$80,000
				59 years	$160,000
				65 years	$320,000

PAY YOURSELF FIRST: THE POWER OF THE HABIT

One of the things I talk to my clients about is the one person who never gets paid. Guess who that is? You. I teach the discipline of *paying yourself first* because, though often neglected, it is the key to a healthy relationship with money. **The three reasons I hear most for not being able to save are:** *I don't make enough money, I'll save what's left after I pay the bills,* and *I have too much debt.* Let's take a look at these excuses one at a time because *paying yourself first* is a mindset and a habit that has nothing to do with the size of your paycheck.

Reason #1: I don't make enough money.

There are two kinds of people—those who save now and those who wait. The employee who makes $1,000 a month and gets in the habit of putting $25 of it away will have $300 saved by the end of the year. The same employee who *waits* until they can "save more" will have zero dollars. Ten years and several pay raises later, they still won't have anything saved.

> Get into the habit of setting aside a portion of what you make now.

It doesn't matter how little; it can be five dollars or five hundred. The important thing is to get in the habit. Bump up that amount annually by 3 percent or $25 a check as your pay increases, and in ten years *you'll be saving $250 a paycheck.* But it will never add up like that unless you get started.

Reason #2: I'll save what's left after I pay the bills.

And what's left is nothing. It happens to everyone. *Saving won't happen if you approach it this way.* It is human nature to spend what is there, so don't even give yourself the option.

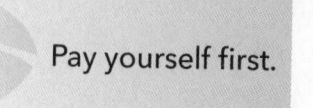

Pay yourself first.

Take out the amount first, before you've even seen it. Have it automatically deducted if you can, and put it into a separate account. Once you get in the habit of doing this, you won't even miss it.

Reason #3: I have too much debt.

Debt won't go away unless you pay it off and nothing will get saved unless you start now. So split the difference. Come up with a formula that you can live with using these three components:

- An amount you can live off—80 percent

- An amount to save—10 percent

- An amount to go towards debt—10 percent.

If you need every penny, the breakdown can be 98 percent, 1 percent, 1 percent. What happens when the debt is gone? You'll be able to increase your savings without having to change your lifestyle or spend a penny more.

Developing the discipline of saving is the hard part. Those who do it now are those who have later success with money. Paying yourself first is a prime example of the hard/easy principle we talked about earlier. Every day you face important financial decisions. Commit to doing the *hard* things now, and the rest will come *easy* later. Conversely, doing the easy things now makes the rest of life hard.

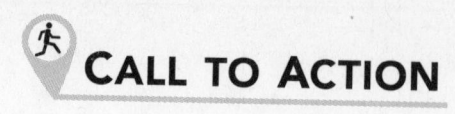

CALL TO ACTION

Create your own money funnel.

- Calculate the amount of money you spend every week eating out or having a drink after work. Replace a percentage of those expenses by cooking and enjoying libations at home.

- Look into refinancing your mortgage interest rates (investigate first and second mortgage options).

- Request refinance of interest rates on credit cards.

- Refinance your insurance premiums—home, auto, and life.

- Reduce your cell phone, Internet, and utility bills by renegotiating new rates or billing plans.

- Identify *exactly* where that additional money will go. Which bucket will you fund first? Your money needs a place to go as defined by you and your RichLife goals.

Bonus Gift: Download your free copy of The RichLife Action Guide at www.RichLifeActionGuide.com.

Chapter 12

HOW TO HAMMER DEBT

"Close to half of all Americans have more credit card debt than savings."
–2014 CBS News *Money Watch*

Does your debt seem so big you don't even know where to begin? Or maybe you know what you *should* be doing, but still you're not doing it? You are not alone in this. A 2012 study by the National Bureau of Economic Research found that 50 percent of all Americans would struggle if they had to come up with an extra $2,000 for an unexpected expense. Most Americans also report at least $1,000 in credit card debt.

DESTROYING OUR DEBT

The time has come to roll up your sleeves, get out the sledge hammer, and work out with some numbers. When it comes to debt, sometimes it can be hard to get started because all together the problem seems so *big*. A lot of people tell me they don't know where to start. Here's the answer: *Go for what will give you the quickest gratification.*

The following strategy will allow you to accomplish something tangible in the least amount of time. It will also get you in the habit of setting aside a portion of your income every month for debt reduction. To help keep you motivated, keep the following principle in mind: If you do the hard thing now, it will be easier later.

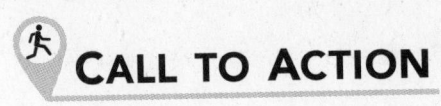
CALL TO ACTION

Step #1: Take a good look at where you stand now.

Make a list of debts. Include credit cards, personal loans, auto loans, student loans, and mortgages. Write down the name of the institution that holds your debt ("Visa Card" is fine) and the amount currently owed.

_____

_____

_____

_____

_____

_____

_____

_____

_____

_____

_____

_____

_____

_____

Step #2: Go for the easy payoff!

What is the amount of your smallest debt?

_____

Step #3: Commit to a number.

What is a realistic amount you can pay extra on this debt while paying minimum payments on all other debts?

_____

Step #4: Where can this money come from?

Using your income and expense sheet created above, look for one area where you can cut down your expenses. For example, if you need an extra $100 a month, maybe all you need to do is cut out the five trips to Starbucks every week and bring a thermos of coffee from home.

_____

_____

_____

_____

_____

_____

_____

Step #5: Stay committed.

Reward yourself each month that you meet your debt reduction goal. Come up with a reward system that you look forward to and one that you can afford. For example, each month after you write the check for your Visa card, reward yourself with half an hour of an activity you love, such as reading a book, sewing, or talking on the phone. Write your reward in the space provided.

_____

_____

_____

_____

_____

Step #6: Repeat Steps 1-5 with the next smallest debt in line.

_____

_____

_____

_____

_____

Bonus Gift: Download your free copy of The RichLife Action Guide at www.RichLifeActionGuide.com.

Chapter 13

THE FIVE THIEVES THAT CAN STEAL YOUR RICHLIFE

To increase your chances of winning you
have to decrease your chances of losing.

Most financial professionals can help you with your investments, but what happens when the unexpected happens? As mentioned earlier, having a RichLife security system in place will help you prepare for the worst while setting you up to enjoy the peace of mind that comes from being prepared.

THE RICHLIFE SECURITY SYSTEM

Enjoying your RichLife will not be possible if every penny of it remains at risk. So what can you do to minimize risk and restore your peace of mind?

In the same way that loan officers perform credit and asset checks, we can take a closer look at your assets and set policies in place to make sure that what you have already built up is secured. We can also ensure the security of any financial plan that we build together. Designing your own personal security system includes fortifying yourself against the following five thieves:

Thief #1: Market Loss

A few years after her daughter, Natasha, was born, my friend Diane bought a 529 plan for her college education. A 529 plan is a tax-deferred plan, similar to a 401(k), that allows you to save money for your children's college tuition. Diane continued contributing to the plan throughout Natasha's childhood, even when it wasn't easy. In fact, there were months when she had to lower her own standard of living to make that payment, but she still gave faithfully every month.

In 2008, just when her daughter was just about to graduate high school, the market fell apart. Natasha's college account suddenly dropped to half of its value at the moment when she needed it most. Diane had done everything right, but it didn't protect her daughter's future. Half of everything she had so carefully put aside for Natasha's college education was wiped out.

Market risk isn't just a problem for retirement accounts. It's a problem for anyone saving for a long-term goal. Most people aren't even aware of the risk their savings are exposed to until it's too late. The only way to protect against this thief is to *take proactive action*. You must prepare for this thief *before* he strikes. Afterward, it will be too late.

CALL TO ACTION

- **Properly Allocate and Diversify Your Assets:** It's vitally important for anyone within a 10-year window of their goal to take a close look at the amount of risk their investment are exposed to. Do you feel your portfolio is adequately diversified? If the market took a drop tomorrow what percent of your assets would suffer a loss? Are you comfortable with that?

- **Periodically Rebalance Your Assets**: Your assets should be rebalanced annually in order to ensure proper diversification. Rebalancing must be performed regularly because as your portfolio grows, it will naturally pull itself out of whack. When one piece of the pie grows bigger than its allotted allocation, you want to move and reinvest that portion into a different piece of the pie to keep your diversification intact.

- **Avoid Emotional Investing**: Proper asset allocation and periodic rebalancing are natural cures to the emotional knee-jerk reaction to unexpected loss. When you are aware of exactly how much risk your assets are exposed to, you won't be surprised by an unexpected loss of money. Periodic balancing allows you to take advantage of the proven model of buy low and sell high, which is exactly what you want to do to take advantage of the most growth potential.

Thief #2: Taxes

Our second thief is very stealthy and can take on many disguises. Erosion factors such as taxes, fees, and inflation eat away at a person's net worth almost invisibly over time, in the end causing substantial losses. On the surface, these things may appear to be inevitable. After all, taxes need to be paid and who can fight against inflation? While protection against the first thief involved proactive steps, fighting against tax thieves is even trickier. It requires using multiple strategies.

In this present economy, laws are changing, tax codes are changing, and the market is changing—so much change so fast that we don't know where inflation will be a year from now or what the tax rates will be. *Because of this uncertainty, it makes sense to think about tax diversification.* Most financial planners focus on diversifying your portfolio, but consider this: if you have 100 percent of your retirement savings in a 401(k), then 100 percent of your savings is taxable. Chances are taxes will go up. Will they be higher when you need to access your money?

Tax diversification is a lot like diversifying your assets. It basically means giving yourself more than one option when it comes to paying the taxes on your lifetime of earned savings.

Understanding the basics of tax diversification begins with a little bit of education.

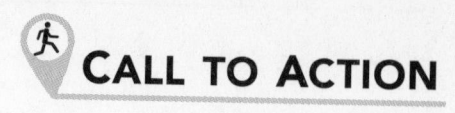

CALL TO ACTION

Understand Your Pre-Tax Investments

Most people fail to realize that by taking advantage of their company's 401(k) plan or traditional IRAs, they are building a big bucket of taxable money. This is money sitting in a giant pot, and it hasn't been taxed yet. It will be taxed when you take this money out, either now or later. It might make sense to take control of when you pay taxes on this money. Why? Because Uncle Sam wants his share. If your money is growing in a traditional IRA, there are many rules and penalties that dictate when and how this money can be withdrawn. *People who enjoy the most success with money understand that they make more money by paying less in taxes.* It might make sense to diversify some of the money in your retirement funds and pay some taxes now in order to enjoy tax-advantaged investment strategies later.

Choose Tax Deferred Investments

Some investments are taxed on their gains while they grow, while other investments are not. Investments that are allowed to grow without being taxed are called tax-deferred investments and they take advantage of compound interest and accumulated growth. Let's look at a hypothetical example to illustrate this point. A dollar that doubles annually and is allowed to grow *without tax* will grow to a sizable investment of $1,048,567 over the course of 20 years. That same dollar allowed to double but taxed at 28 percent annually will only grow to $51,353. Now you see why utilizing the right tax strategies is so crucial.

Utilize Tax-Free Distribution Strategies Where Appropriate

There are investment vehicles such as Roth IRAs and cash value life insurance when structured properly that allow for tax free distribution. This means that when you take this money out at some future date, no taxes are owed. It often makes a lot of sense to create tax-free distribution strategies as a part of your complete financial strategy. Traditional IRAs can also be converted to Roth IRAs, converting a taxable bucket of money into a tax-free bucket of money. To determine the right mix, analysis needs to be done based on your goals, timeline, tax bracket, and other variables.

Thief #3: Critical Illness

No one ever thinks there's a chance his or her life could be shattered by one of the Big Three:

- Cancer

- Heart Attack

- Stroke

We all think, "That's not going to happen to me." Honestly, even though I know the statistics, I often think it won't happen to me either. Here's the hard truth: If you're married, statistics say that there's a good chance one of the Big Three will strike. The Centers for Disease Control and Prevention (CDC) reported in 2009 that 75 percent of people over 40 experienced a critical illness at some point during their lives. What you need to be prepared for is that surviving one of the Big Three could become your biggest problem.

The number one cause of bankruptcy in the U.S. is surviving a critical illness.[1] When the rent or mortgage payments cannot be met, families face losing their homes. Relationships become strained and the quality of life becomes greatly compromised. Add to that the fact that medical bills continue to pile up and you have a real recipe for disaster. The accounts you have set up for other purposes such as college and retirement become tapped. You would gladly spend all of it ten times over to insure the health and well-being of a loved one, but after all is said and done, where does this leave you and your family with regard to your RichLife?

If you don't plan for this you're wide open to having your future destroyed. This is why planning for critical illness is part of a solid financial foundation. Without a contingency plan in place, just one major medical event could wipe out your entire future.

CALL TO ACTION

- **Replacement Income Plan:** If you or your spouse is unable to work for a period of time due to a critical illness, do you have a plan in place to replace this lost income?

- **A Way to Pay for Extensive Treatment:** When chronic illness such as cancer strikes, the treatment is often long term and costly. How will you pay for this treatment? For most middle class Americans, health insurance offers little protection against the costs of paying for chronic illness.[2] Will you have to cash in your 401(k) or borrow against your house? Or do you have a contingency plan in place?

Thief #4: Cost of Long Term Care

If you are near or entering retirement age, funding long term care is one area you will also want to pay close attention to. Disability affects 69 percent of people who live to be in their 90s, and the cost of proper care can quickly deplete your financial resources.[3] Even if you are in excellent health now, it's important to consider the changes that might be coming down the road. *Statistics reveal that 70 percent of 65-year-olds today will need some form of long term care, and 20 percent of those cases will require care for five years or longer.*[4]

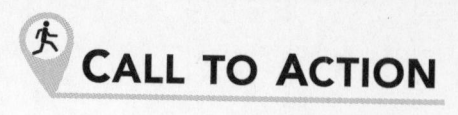

CALL TO ACTION

- **Do You Have the Right Kind of Life Insurance?** Many newer life insurance products offer critical care riders and living benefits to help cover the costs of long term care. These are benefits you can access while you are still living to help pay for the increasing costs of long term care. If no long term care is needed, the benefit is paid out to your beneficiaries.

- **Is it Too Late to Qualify for Long Term Care Insurance?** Many companies offer long term care insurance that functions much like the insurance policies for your home or car. If you end up not needing long term care, there is no benefit paid out to you or your beneficiaries, but you do get peace of mind. The older you get the more difficult and expensive it becomes to qualify for traditional long term care insurance.

Thief #5: Premature Death

No one likes to think about dying. Because of this, many families are caught short when premature death does occur. Accidents, disease, or illness can take the breadwinner out of the picture and leave the survivors in a financially compromised position. We don't ever want to think about something like that happening, but death is the one thing in our lives that we can count on happening. No one is excluded. It only makes sense to be prepared.

This subject takes on a very personal note with me because my own father died at age forty-nine. He had a successful business, but that was of little use to my mother after he was gone. My father had been diligent to invest back into his retail nursery business, but he had omitted the simple step of purchasing enough life insurance. As a result, my mother's day-to-day life became much more difficult after he passed away.

During times of transition such as divorce or death, people are at their most vulnerable, both emotionally and financially. These times are when *money is in motion,* and critical decisions often have to be made. If there is not a trusted financial professional able to help them who has their best interests in mind, there's a good chance an irreversible money mistake will be made. This is a scenario I've seen repeated many times over the years. I urge you not to take this advice lightly. So many people have learned the hard way, but you don't have to.

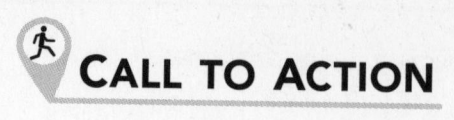

CALL TO ACTION

- **Educate Yourself About Your Options:** A lot of families think they can't afford life insurance. Are you educated about all your options? Make sure you understand the difference between whole life and term policies before making your purchase. A qualified financial professional can help explain your options.

- **Review Any Policies That Are Already in Place:** In the same way that you test the batteries on your smoke alarm, these policies must also be tested against your current lifestyle situation. Things change; shift happens. Come marriage, divorce, or birth, you want the peace of mind knowing that if something happened, your family will keep their RichLife intact.

- **Begin the Process of Searching for a Financial Professional.** It's important to meet with an attorney and to have a will in place before the event of death. A qualified financial professional can help you accomplish all your objectives. Start with references from family and friends. Use the Internet as a tool and check out their profile and company information on sites such as LinkedIn.

NOTES

1. "Biggest Cause of Personal Bankruptcy: Medical Bills," TODAY.com, accessed January 15, 2016, http://www.today .com/money/biggest-cause-personal-bankruptcy-medical-bills-6C10442408.

2. Catherine Arnst, "Study Links Medical Costs and Personal Bankruptcy," Bloomberg Business Week, June 04, 2009, http://www.businessweek.com/bwdaily/dnflash/content/ jun2009/db2009064_666715.htm.

3. "Who Needs Care?" Longtermcare.gov, accessed January 15, 2016, http://longtermcare.gov/the-basics/who-needs-care.

4. "How Much Care Will You Need?" Longtermcare.gov, accessed January 15, 2016, http://longtermcare.gov/ the-basics/how-much-care-will-you-need.

Bonus Gift: Download your free copy of The RichLife Action Guide at www.RichLifeActionGuide.com.

Chapter 14

How Much Insurance Do I Really Need? The DIME Analysis

How much protection is enough?

The funny thing about accumulating money is that the more of it you have, the more you feel yourself to be at risk. This is true of all our financial assets and most of the physical ones as well, including our homes, our cars, and our lifestyle. The more you have, the more you stand to lose. The strategies for risk transfer are often the most neglected and underutilized aspects of a financial plan, yet they are a necessary component when creating a sound foundation.

Risk transfer is what it sounds like—you take the risk factor and you transfer that responsibility to somebody else, so if something bad happens, you don't have to pay. Such risks might include hardship due to death, disability, or critical illness. How much protection do you need?

BUYING BY THE DIME: UNDERSTANDING YOUR NEEDS

How do you arrive at a realistic number when it comes to protecting the people you love? Use the DIME method to figure out how much protection you want and need and how much you can afford.

- **D** is for Debts. These are the credit cards and car payments that will still need to be paid off in the event of your spouse's death. (This category does not include the mortgage.)

- **I** is for Income. This is the amount of money the household generates. Look at both the amounts brought in by you and your spouse. These amounts might be different. You need to be prepared for the loss of either. How many years of income would you like to provide for your loved ones in the event of your death?

- **M** is for Mortgage. There are many financial products specifically designed to pay off the mortgage in the event of spousal death. Depending on your financial situation and the kind of mortgage you have, this might be an important consideration for you.

- **E is for Education.** Do you have kids who want to go to college? Will they need your help paying for college? Do you have a plan for this?

CALL TO ACTION

To calculate how much insurance you need, give the DIME method a try.

- Add up your debts (example: $18,000).

- Calculate your income and multiply that by 3, 5, or 10 years depending on the number of years of your income that you would like to replace (example, $30,000 x 5 = $150,000).

- Mortgage amount owed (example: $140,000)

- Estimate education expenses (example: $250,000)

  TOTAL: $558,000.

This is the amount of insurance coverage you need in order to cover your goals and objectives.

Bonus Gift: Download your free copy of The RichLife Action Guide at www.RichLifeActionGuide.com.

Chapter 15

SWOT YOUR FINANCES

"Don't be afraid of enemies who attack you.
Be afraid of the friends who flatter you."
—DALE CARNEGIE

This chapter has been focused on gathering data to produce an accurate snapshot of where you are now with regard to your money. The final step to this process involves gathering data of a different sort—we're going to take an inside look at the positive and negative attributes that may affect your monetary goals. As the above quote suggests, when it comes to realistic assessment, honesty is your friend.

One tool used by businesses of all sizes and shapes is the SWOT analysis. Developed to identify the opposition inherent to any new goal or venture, SWOT is an acronym for Strengths, Weaknesses, Opportunities, and Threats. While it is most commonly employed as an assessment or brainstorming tool for organizations, the SWOT analysis can also be used to take a fearless look at the resources and options available to you as an individual or household member.

Each of the four boxes relates to the others, and they are placed side by side for comparison. This gives you the ability to take a realistic look at your strengths with your finances, as well as a way to identify your weaknesses. We also look at your opportunities and your threats. Recording your answers in each of the four areas allows you to see clearly what needs to be addressed, changed, and improved. It also helps you to see what is already working so you can capitalize on those strengths. In short, the SWOT analysis is a valuable tool that can help you gain clarity about your finances, moving you one step closer to the achievement of your RichLife.

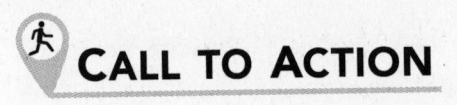
CALL TO ACTION

Invite each individual involved in the handling, earning, spending, and saving of money to fill out each of the four boxes below. You are welcome to make copies of this page in the book, or simply use a blank piece of paper with the appropriate headings. There are no wrong answers in a SWOT analysis, but strive for honesty and clarity as much as possible in each of the four areas.

STRENGTHS	WEAKNESSES
OPPORTUNITIES	THREATS

Bonus Gift: Download your free copy of The RichLife Action Guide at www.RichLifeActionGuide.com.

Chapter 16

YOUR RICHLIFE COMMITMENTS

"It's a basic fact of life that many things
'everybody knows' turn out to be wrong."
—JIM ROGERS

A lot of people have a lot of funny ideas about money. It is either the key to their happiness or the root of all evil, or somewhere in between. A lot of the things we have been taught about money simply aren't true. The truth is, money is neither good nor bad. Money by itself is neutral. *This is because money is a tool designed to serve us, not the other way around.*

It's what you do with money that dictates its value. As a financial professional, I want to see that you are financially secure, yes, but more than that I want you to live a fulfilled life. When clients come to me for help with their finances, those who have invested in their human assets end up doing far better in the end than those who don't, even if at first their finances are in shambles. This points to the larger truth that of the three asset classes, human, physical, and financial, only humans have the ability to create the other two.

> **It is people who are the real asset, not the money they make.**

The most valuable legacy you can leave behind for your children, your family, and the world at large *is a life well lived.*

⚐ CALL TO ACTION

I Want to Know: Complete the following worksheets by diligently answering the following questions. Go to www .beauhenderson.com and share your goals, concerns and commitments to moving toward your definition of a RichLife."

Chapter One: The Realities of Hard/Easy.

My take away from this chapter was:

_____

_____

_____

_____

_____

_____

_____

_____

_____

_____

_____

_____

_____

_____

_____

_____

_____

_____

_____

Here is my commitment for this chapter:

_____

_____

_____

_____

_____

_____

_____

_____

_____

_____

_____

_____

_____

_____

_____

Chapter Two: Welcome to Life School.

My take away from this chapter was:

_____

_____

_____

_____

_____

_____

_____

_____

_____

_____

_____

_____

_____

_____

_____

_____

_____

Here is my commitment for this chapter:

_____

_____

_____

_____

_____

_____

_____

_____

_____

_____

_____

_____

_____

_____

_____

_____

Chapter Three: An Attitude of Gratitude.

My take away from this chapter was:

_____

_____

_____

_____

_____

_____

_____

_____

_____

_____

_____

_____

_____

_____

_____

Here is my commitment for this chapter:

_____

_____

_____

_____

_____

_____

_____

_____

_____

_____

_____

_____

_____

Chapter Four: Start with the Why: What's Your Definition of a RichLife?

My take away from this chapter was:

_____

_____

_____

_____

_____

_____

_____

_____

_____

_____

_____

_____

_____

_____

Here is my commitment for this chapter:

_____

_____

_____

_____

_____

_____

_____

_____

_____

_____

_____

_____

_____

_____

_____

_____

Chapter Five: The When I, Then I Game.

My take away from this chapter was:

_____

_____

_____

_____

_____

_____

_____

_____

_____

_____

_____

_____

_____

_____

_____

Here is my commitment for this chapter:

_____

_____

_____

_____

_____

_____

_____

_____

_____

_____

_____

_____

_____

_____

Chapter Six: The DISC Personality Profile.

My take away from this chapter was:

_____

_____

_____

_____

_____

_____

_____

_____

_____

_____

_____

_____

_____

_____

_____

_____

Here is my commitment for this chapter:

_____

_____

_____

_____

_____

_____

_____

_____

_____

_____

_____

_____

_____

_____

_____

_____

Chapter Seven: Investing in Human Assets.

My take away from this chapter was:

_____

_____

_____

_____

_____

_____

_____

_____

_____

_____

_____

_____

_____

_____

_____

_____

_____

Here is my commitment for this chapter:

_____

_____

_____

_____

_____

_____

_____

_____

_____

_____

_____

_____

_____

_____

_____

Chapter Eight: The SMART Goal System.

My take away from this chapter was:

_____

_____

_____

_____

_____

_____

_____

_____

_____

_____

_____

_____

_____

_____

_____

_____

_____

Here is my commitment for this chapter:

_____

_____

_____

_____

_____

_____

_____

_____

_____

_____

_____

_____

_____

_____

Chapter Nine: Contribution.

My take away from this chapter was:

_____

_____

_____

_____

_____

_____

_____

_____

_____

_____

_____

_____

_____

_____

_____

_____

Here is my commitment for this chapter:

_____

_____

_____

_____

_____

_____

_____

_____

_____

_____

_____

_____

_____

_____

_____

_____

_____

Chapter Ten: Know Your Numbers.

My take away from this chapter was:

_____

_____

_____

_____

_____

_____

_____

_____

_____

_____

_____

_____

_____

_____

_____

_____

Here is my commitment for this chapter:

_____

_____

_____

_____

_____

_____

_____

_____

_____

_____

_____

_____

_____

_____

_____

_____

Chapter Eleven: How Real People Save Money.

My take away from this chapter was:

_____

_____

_____

_____

_____

_____

_____

_____

_____

_____

_____

_____

_____

_____

_____

_____

Here is my commitment for this chapter:

_____

_____

_____

_____

_____

_____

_____

_____

_____

_____

_____

_____

_____

_____

_____

_____

Chapter Twelve: How to Hammer Credit Card Debt.

My take away from this chapter was:

_____

_____

_____

_____

_____

_____

_____

_____

_____

_____

_____

_____

_____

_____

_____

Here is my commitment for this chapter:

_____

_____

_____

_____

_____

_____

_____

_____

_____

_____

_____

_____

_____

_____

_____

_____

_____

Chapter Thirteen: The Five Thieves That Can Steal Your RichLife.

My take away from this chapter was:

_____

_____

_____

_____

_____

_____

_____

_____

_____

_____

_____

_____

_____

_____

Here is my commitment for this chapter:

_____

_____

_____

_____

_____

_____

_____

_____

_____

_____

_____

_____

_____

_____

_____

Chapter Fourteen: How Much Insurance Do I Really Need?

My take away from this chapter was:

_____

_____

_____

_____

_____

_____

_____

_____

_____

_____

_____

_____

_____

_____

_____

_____

_____

Here is my commitment for this chapter:

_____

_____

_____

_____

_____

_____

_____

_____

_____

_____

_____

_____

_____

_____

_____

_____

Bonus Gift: Download your free copy of The RichLife Action Guide at www.RichLifeActionGuide.com.

CONGRATULATIONS!!!

You have completed the Roadmap to a RichLife. Now it's time to take the first step!

Share your top goals and your definition of a RichLife at www.BeauHenderson.com

BONUS MATERAL FROM

Ten Investments for True Wealth

BEAU HENDERSON

Investment #6

MASTER YOUR MONEY MAP

"In macroeconomics, success or failure is not
due to the performance of the investment. It is
always due to the efficiency of the investor."
—ANDREW ROSENBAUM, author of
The Wealth Swing Coach

YOU ARE HERE!

We are now at the halfway point of the book and the time has come to talk about some basic financial principles. We are going to get started by taking a look at where you are with regard to your finances. When using a GPS system in your car to map out a road trip, you must have two pieces of information. First, *you must know your destination*—or where you are going. Second, and equally as important, *you must know where you are now*. This is your starting point. Without knowing those two pieces of information—your present position and your destination—there's no way you can map a course.

Your RichLife is where you are going. But before we can get you there, we must figure out where you are right now with regard to money. A lot of people don't want to take a close look at their finances. They either don't have the time, think it will be too depressing, or are afraid of the changes that may be required of them. The truth is, *not* looking at your finances causes much more of an energy drain than the time it takes to get clear about your numbers. And you won't be able to reach your end destination with any certainty without a clear starting point.

Let's look at it another way. If you go into a shopping mall and you want to go to McDonald's, the first thing you do is locate the mall directory stationed at the main entrance. On the directory you'll find a little red star that says, "You are here!" Only then can you figure out which direction to go to get to McDonald's. Without that little red star, any movement you made would be inefficient. Any direction you chose would be a random shot in the dark. You might walk for hours, wasting all your energy going in the exact opposite direction. You might stumble on the store eventually, but you'd have no idea how you did it. You wouldn't be able to get there again with any certainty, and you wouldn't be able to help anybody else get there. When this metaphor is applied to your life and finances, we could be talking about years of poor money management and hundreds of thousands of dollars spent inefficiently.

Taking a good look at where you are now is the first step in mapping out the journey for a successful financial future. Most people are just hoping things will work out. They figure if they work hard and keep at it, the money will take care of itself. In my career as a financial advisor, I have seen scores of business owners and individuals who appear successful and on top of their game, but do not know exactly what is coming in and what is going out on any given month. If you are nodding your head, you are not alone. The overwhelming majority of people do not know where they stand with their finances.

ON SIGHT

When Shawn and his wife Krista started their photography business, they were excited to have identified a specific niche—on location photography for students involved in sports. They named their company On Sight, invested in a professional, high-resolution printer, and set up a slick online ordering system for the parents. It was the beginning of hockey season in the upper Midwest, and they were booked solid, shooting games every weekend and downloading the photographs to their website. Shawn focused on the photography, taking the pictures, fine-tuning and cropping the images, and constantly updating the website. Krista secured future bookings and managed the printing and shipment of the orders.

The business took off right away. Shawn's pictures were good and their price point was in line with what parents were willing to pay. The hours Shawn spent in the ice arenas began to pay off. By the end of their first month, On Sight had an impressive amount of capital flowing into their bank account. One afternoon, the president of the bank himself came out to meet Shawn in the lobby. They shook hands and he congratulated Shawn on the success of the business. By the end of their first year, Shawn and Krista had deposited more than $300,000 in funds, and On Sight was deemed a huge success.

As the season for winter sports started up again the following year, Shawn booked himself and his wife on a flight to Colorado where they would shoot several high-profile skiing events. The gig would look impressive on their website and was a big, three-day weekend event. But when Shawn charged the plane tickets to his business credit card, the transaction was unexpectedly declined.

"I had no idea how it happened. We were making so much money, it didn't seem possible that we could have spent more than what was coming in. But we were so focused on the success of the company, we said 'yes' to everything, every booking, every engagement, and every opportunity. We never stopped to look at what it would cost and to ask if there was enough in our budget. We didn't even *have* a budget!"

MICRO VERSES MACRO

In the case of Shawn and Krista, a budget wasn't what they needed. A lot of people make the mistake of thinking that creating a budget is the first step when really it is only a tool. A budget can only help you if you know where you are and where you want to go. In other words, *you must have the whole picture.* What happened with On Sight is a common business mistake that I have seen many times. Decisions about money are made in the moment, *based on what is easiest or cheapest now* as opposed to what will create a more favorable future. This short-sighted view of money is called *microeconomics.* Money is spent or saved without considering future repercussions or how it affects the picture as a whole.

Going back to our shopping analogy, micro-decisions would be buying the cheap, disposable versions of things instead of investing in lasting, more permanent options. It will result in the need to buy that item again, which requires more of your time and more of your assets. While sometimes it does make sense to save a few bucks today and buy the cheaper item, *the micro view of money often leads to an erosion of financial stability over the long term.* This is because every financial decision *does* affect the picture of the whole. Seemingly little mistakes over time add up to big errors. They can go undetected and eat away at your future unless you take the time now to focus on your numbers.

Without identifying both your starting point and your destination, your money decisions won't be grounded. You will be adrift, directionless, and at the mercy of the economy. You will be reacting instead of directing your life. We can think of the micro/macro model as the difference between staying focused on the raft versus focused on the shore. With the micro view of money, all that matters is the raft, or where you are today. You only take care of the raft, and so your direction is left to the mercy of the river. The river can be likened to the economy. When it is rough, you will be having a miserable ride. When things are going well, the sailing will be smooth. Either way, it's vital to the health of your financial future to know where, exactly, you are headed.

With the macro view of money, your focus is on the end goal of reaching shore. You need to take care of your raft and stay current on repairs, yes. But decisions about whether or not to invest in the raft will be calculated based on how much further you have to go. It wouldn't make sense to buy a sail, for example, if you are so close to land that all you have to do is hop out and drag the raft onto the sand.

Going back to the business started by Shawn and Krista, had they started with the bigger picture in mind, they would have managed their income differently. The trouble here was that they never took the time to identify what that bigger picture was. The general idea of success and knowing how much money is coming into the bank is not the same thing as a money map. In the end, Shawn and

Krista did file for bankruptcy. Together they owed a mind-boggling amount of money in business credit card debt and loans. They were paying the bills from last month with what they were earning at the current booking and had no idea where they stood financially at any given point. With their microeconomic view—no plan and no budget—they took on too much too soon, and found themselves in way over their heads.

KNOW YOUR NUMBERS

Beginning with the end in mind and knowing what is coming in and what is going out is more than just good advice—*it's essential to reaching your destination.* Most people have a little money tucked away in savings; others may have done a little investing in mutual funds or real estate. Some people live on a fixed income or receive regular paychecks, while others work on a per project basis, receiving sales commissions. But none of the numbers are concrete. The income and expenses for each month are unknown. For the most part, people are just *hoping* that everything works out all right. This strategy—if you can call it that—is as follows: "I've done a little here and a little there. And I work hard. *I hope* when I get to the time of financial need at some point in the future, it will all just work out."

When it comes to prosperity, hoping doesn't cut it. It sets up the conditions of wanting something that isn't there, and these conditions are then perpetuated through simple avoidance or ignorance. Hoping puts someone else in charge. Knowing puts you in the driver's seat. Even if you have no gift for numbers, there is no reason why you can't take charge of your finances today. In order to create the conditions favorable to reaching your desired destination, you must begin with where you are now, and that means doing the work of learning how much money is coming in, how much is going out, the total of your assets, and the total of your liabilities. Just like using a GPS system or entering a shopping mall, without a starting point any movement made toward your destination will be inefficient and at best a gamble. Why take such an unnecessary risk when you don't have to? When it comes to financial success, you need to bite the bullet now and do the work to create your Money Map. This map will tell you where you are financially, and from there you can drive your life forward to wherever it is you want to go.

I am happy to say that Shawn and Krista have their act together now. They recovered, learned their lesson from life school, and took the time to restructure and map out their finances instead of focusing solely on the income. It doesn't matter if you're earning one hundred dollars or one million if that same amount is being spent simultaneously. Shawn and Krista started over, and this time they have the big picture, *with both a beginning and an end point in mind.*

CREATING YOUR MONEY MAP

The first step to creating your Money Map is to work on two important financial statements—your balance sheet and your income statement. The balance sheet will give you a snapshot in time, so to speak, showing you where you stand with regard to assets and liabilities. Your income statement shows you the cash flow, or what is coming in and going out in any given month. These two statements together give you an accurate reading of where you stand financially. For most people, this work is not fun and the reality is that most personality types will never even do this exercise. The good news, however, is that the work doesn't have to be done by *you.*

Be honest with yourself here. I'm a financial planner and even though I work with numbers for a living, I pay someone a monthly fee to keep my receipts and expenses current with my income. If the thought of working on financial statements makes your skin crawl, that's okay! There are people out there who do this kind of work. There are people for whom bookkeeping is their life purpose. Many of my clients pay a bookkeeper as little as $100 a month to deliver current financial statements. For individuals who run their own business and keep track of daily receipts and expenditures, having this kind of service done for you can be a lifesaver. Others might select a one-time fee and have someone show them how or install a service such as QuickBooks™. Or they might learn how to do it themselves by spending some time online with tools such as Mint°, Microsoft Money, or YNAB™ (You Need a Budget). For others, the situation might best be served by a good old-fashioned ledger book and pencil.

It doesn't matter how you do it. It only matters that it gets done. In order to achieve financial success, *you need to know your numbers.* Delegate the task if it is something that is not your strength. Knowing your numbers will put you ahead of over 90 percent of your peers and competitors and will help you map out the path to your definition of a fulfilling financial future based on certainty, not luck.

CASH FLOW IS KING

Your **income statement** will have two sides, one side with what comes in, or income, and the other side with what goes out, or expenses. To get a clear idea of what is going out, look at your credit card statements as well as your paper receipts. Include necessary expenses such as fuel for both your car and yourself, and any monthly bills for things such as your phone and Internet, car and health insurance. Also include a category for repairs and maintenance. Factor in an amount that will cover regular oil changes and other maintenance procedures including new tires. Create yet another miscellaneous category to include unexpected expenses such as birthday presents and gifts

Keeping track of your income will be different for everybody in that some of us have steady salaries and predictable paychecks, while others don't. If you are self-employed, work on a commission basis, or have seasonal employment, your income will need to be based on an average. To find that number will require a little bit of digging, but it will be worth it. Calculate your average monthly income by looking at last year's taxes, or by factoring in all income streams, even those whose yields are unpredictable, and dividing by twelve to find an average. Having a number like that can help you put aside the correct amount of money during times of heavy cash flow to cover during the leaner months.

The next financial statement, a **balance sheet**, will calculate your net worth. Your net worth will change over longer periods of time, as the value of what you own increases or decreases depending on the market, and more of your loans are paid off, decreasing your liability. The balance sheet will help give you an accurate picture of where you stand with regard to *what you own and what you owe* using two categories, *assets* and *liabilities*. Assets are those physical items you own which have a calculated worth in dollars. They include vehicles, real estate, and tools or equipment. Liabilities would include all financial obligations which must be met every month such as the mortgage and loan payments. If your business is *renting* a space, then it is not liable for the rent should the business decide to fold or change locations. The monthly rent would be listed as an "expense" and calculated as a bill. If the business *owns* its place of operation, then this building would be an asset, increasing its overall net worth. If the business has a *loan* for the building it owns, then the property would be listed as both an asset and a liability, the building being the asset and the mortgage or loan being the liability. Over time, the balance would shift as you make payments. You will own more of the property as you pay off the principal of the loan, decreasing your liability while increasing your assets.

Once you have tallied the numbers, take a look at the totals. How much is coming in each month? How much is going out? If you need an extra $100 a month to put aside for a college fund, maybe all you need to do is cut out the five trips to Starbucks every week and bring a thermos of coffee from home. Maybe some of your assets have turned into liabilities you can't really afford. Or maybe you are in better shape than you thought you would be. The bottom line is—*now you know.*

BORROWING A LIFESTYLE

When Paul's wife passed away at the age of thirty-six, he went into a tailspin of grief. Not only had he lost his life partner and friend, but they'd had a daughter together. Rebecca was only ten, and now she was left without a mother. That thought overwhelmed Paul. He in no way felt prepared to fill the shoes his wife left empty.

At the beginning there were friends and many offers of help. Paul got his daughter through it, taking it day by day. He did whatever it took to get them from point A to point B with as little suffering as possible. If it was raining, he and Rebecca took a cab. If it was a school night and they hadn't eaten dinner, they would go out some place nice. If she needed a dress to wear for a school concert, he ordered one online and had it delivered overnight. Whatever the cost, it didn't matter. Paul was just going through the grieving process, and as the single parent to a young girl, he needed to do it with as much grace and dignity as possible.

A year went by, and then another. Paul was back in the full swing of his life, working a steady and regular job as a property surveyor. Rebecca was now almost a teenager and had taken up an interest in horses. The spending habits he had developed during the past two years didn't change. He bought his daughter a horse they couldn't afford and found a place to board it. She began taking regular riding lessons at $60 an hour, three times a week. Soon after that she wanted to enter her horse in shows, and Paul couldn't say no.

When things started to get tight, Paul financed a home equity line of credit. That gave him and his daughter some breathing room for another year. Meanwhile he continued to spend money so they could have the best of everything. Every two years he bought a newer car; they got another horse so that he could go on rides with her. Eventually they even bought a trailer so she could travel to out-of-state shows.

When things got tight again, he sold a piece of real estate. This went on for ten years until Rebecca graduated from high school and went on to college. With his daughter out of the house, things got very quiet. The retirement years loomed up ahead on the horizon. Paul took a look around at his financial affairs and realized he was in no way prepared. When the property taxes came due, he struggled to make the payment.

"It's this economy!" he complained. "It's a bad market!"

Yet when he finally got all of his finances together and took a look at where he stood, Paul learned that he had been outspending his income for years

LIVE BELOW YOUR MEANS

It is very easy to charge things on a credit card. It is also easy to fall into the trap of trying to impress people with a lifestyle you can't afford. It is human nature to want to give the best to your children, your friends, even to yourself. But the only way to achieve the balance of health and the full wealth of all the assets—human, physical and financial—is by investing in the big picture. Knowing where you are going will keep you from the temptation of borrowing a lifestyle that doesn't take you where you want to go. Even if it is possible to do everything you want to do in the moment and still make it work, as Paul did, in the end you will have nothing left to show for it. You will not get to your final destination.

I have a client who lives on the outskirts of town and works on old rural homes, updating their plumbing. Morgan is a straightforward, blue-collar kind of guy, but with tremendous saving habits. His net worth is two to three times greater than some of my highest earning clients, yet he doesn't dress in designer suits. He also isn't stressed by his lifestyle. One of the more interesting things I've noticed over the years is that the most financially secure people are those who don't feel the need to use their money as leverage. In other words, their appearance doesn't unnecessarily advertise their wealth. Their success allows them to live in a way that suits them, without having to impress others, and they are among the happiest, most easygoing people I know

One thing I ask my clients to do is to envision their lives as they would like to see them ten years from now. Now we did this in a previous chapter with regard to designing your RichLife, but doing so with regard to your finances will help you to develop a *macroeconomic* mindset. Ten years is long enough to accomplish some pretty big things, yet small enough to picture clearly. The time will also go by faster than you'd ever expect it. If you have a clear picture of where you want to be, it becomes easier to say "no" to the things you can't afford now like a new car or a bigger house. You can look at that new car and say, "I'd rather not have a car payment." You can look at that bigger house and say, "I'd rather have the weekend off, kneeling in the dirt and planting tulips with my granddaughter."

Once you have done the work and understand your numbers, it is essential that you live within those means. One of the great secrets to building wealth *is to live below your means*. Even though you *can* go out to dinner, you don't. Even though you *can* afford a higher car payment, you invest that money differently. You put it to work for you so that ten years from now, you achieve the picture of your RichLife. Whether you are earning $150,000 a year or $20,000, you *can* become wealthy if you have more coming in than going out.

We live in a time of plenty—plenty of food, plenty of choices, plenty of credit cards. On any given day we are surrounded by more calories than we need, yet we don't consume them all. We choose instead a diet that will support a healthy body and build a healthy immune system. We say yes to some things and no to others. The doctors tell us to stop eating just before we become too full. As your financial planner, I am telling you the same thing with regard to your money. Choose to stop spending before you have spent everything. Choose to keep things comfortable for yourself by living below your means. This will support a healthy financial future

THE TRUTH ABOUT MONEY

To conclude our chapter about money, I would like to take a close look at what money really is. I've seen a lot of people who are pretty confused about money. They risk everything to get more of it because they believe that it has the power to make them happy. Like Sussil Liyanage from the previous chapter, maybe you have also discovered for yourself that money alone does not give you a complete life.

I admit that money is a powerful word. The promise of it has the ability to make people do and say crazy things. But the bottom line here is that building a truly rich and fulfilled life requires that we keep money in its proper place. We must remember what it really is.

On my radio show and during seminars, I talk a lot about *the truth of dead presidents on paper.* Because really, when it comes right down to it, that's all money is. Money in and of itself has no intrinsic value. It is merely a tool with which to *measure* value. If you have something of value and I want to purchase that item from you, in our society I give you money for it. In America that would be dollars. In Sri Lanka, it would be rupees. In many other parts of the world, it would be euros. In centuries past I might have given you gold doubloons, a pretty shell, a belt of beaded wampum, or even salt. Money is a medium of exchange. To think of money in this way may require a paradigm shift from what you have heard all your life. If you are looking at your income statement and thinking, *I need more money!* that thought likely makes you tense and anxious, so keep in mind where you want to go and what you want to achieve. Remember that money is only a tool and should never take priority over the people it was meant to serve.

Instead of thinking about acquiring money, focus on utilizing your assets and resources to move you toward your goals and objectives. Build on that as your foundation. Money can then have a greater impact on the things in life that are truly fulfilling. It can then be of service to you, instead of you being the one serving it. By viewing money this way, your thoughts about it will undergo a shift. Instead of focusing on accumulating money, you are adding value to your life. My experience is that only the latter can produce long-term financial success and a fulfilled and balanced life.

THE TRUTH ABOUT INVESTMENTS

Another question I get asked a lot concerns what to do with money. Individuals come to me and ask the vague question of, "What is the best investment?" Or they ask me specific questions such as, "Should I invest in stocks? In bonds, gold, real estate, businesses, etc.?"

My answer: In order to know, I'll have to ask you a lot more questions. I need more information."

The value of an investment has to do with the financial goals and objectives of the investor. In other words, there is no best investment.

While most people focus on trying to find the best investment, true success comes when you realize that all investments are *neutral*. It is neither a winner nor a loser for any one person. In fact, two different people can be set up in the exact same investment—one might come out with huge gains and the other end up broke. In other words, each investor begins from a different place, has a different destination in mind, and a different financial IQ. What must be clear from the outset are the particular situations and the long-term objectives of the investor. In other words, each investor *begins from a different place*, and each one has *a different destination* in mind. In order to choose "the best investment," you must be clear about those two things first.

Let's take a look at a case in point. Do you remember my client David from our chapter about clarity? When I asked him *why* he wanted to invest in real estate, his answer was, "Because there are some great deals out there now." He'd been reading about how to pick up foreclosed houses at deep discounts. While this was true, I pressed him further.

"*Why* do you want to invest in real estate?" I continued to present the same question, and he gave me vague answers until he realized he wasn't really getting to the heart of things. His answer wasn't really solid. He thought about it for a minute, and then finally he replied, "I want to invest in real estate because five years from now, I don't want to be working at my job anymore."

Well, now we were getting somewhere. But I wasn't finished. My next question was, "*Why* do you want to retire in five years?" This might sound like an unnecessary question, but everyone has a different idea about what retirement really is. Everyone has an objective in mind, even if they themselves haven't said it out loud. We kept drilling down with more specific questions until it was finally revealed that he needed $3,000 a month to supplement his income so he could stay home and help raise his granddaughter. He had identified caring for and spending time with his granddaughter, at this point in his life, as his new definition of a RichLife.

Now we could begin to map a course for him to reach his goals and objectives. Had we begun investing in real estate without this valuable interchange, things could have gotten way off course. The type of real estate David had been considering would have been totally wrong for his particular situation, and if he had used it he might never have reached his financial objective in the time frame he envisioned. This happens all the time—people hear something on the news or read about it in the newspaper and they're ready to base their investment program on something that "sounds good."

Let's go back to the analogy of using a GPS to map your road trip. Choosing an investment program before you are clear on your objectives is like starting out in Atlanta, Georgia and you want to go to San Diego, California, but instead of heading west you go north toward Buffalo, New York, because you heard on the news it was a great place to visit right now! It makes no sense, yet a lot of people fall for it. With regard to investments, your definition of a RichLife is located at the end of your biggest why.

The best way to map your investment strategy is to ask yourself "why" until you can't ask it any more. This will get you to the heart of your motivation. Once that is identified, you can plan a strategy designed to move you *toward* your desired destination.

IS IT WORTH THE COST?

In the same way that money is neutral and investments are neutral, so too are those things we choose to buy. You might look at your neighbor's boat sitting up on blocks in the backyard and think to yourself, "Wow, what a waste of money." But what if living on a houseboat is their idea of a dream retirement? You can look at any purchases you make with the same paradigm shift we described earlier. Purchasing grown-up toys like boats and snowmobiles is neither good nor bad. They will simply either serve you or not. The purchase will either help move you *toward* your goals or move you *away* from those goals. Looking at purchasing decisions in this way will help make your decisions with clarity instead of judgment.

I would like to leave you with some good advice I learned from my friend and mentor, Steven D'Annunzio. A good rule of thumb to apply to any purchasing decision, be it large or small, is to ask: Is the price worth the cost? In other words, is the price of what I am doing today worth the cost in the future? If you keep the big picture in mind, the answer to that question should help you stay the course toward destination RichLife.

PORTFOLIO BUILDER

We covered some valuable ground in this chapter with regard to finances. I hope you understand the importance of knowing your numbers. Before you can begin moving toward your RichLife, you must first identify where it is you are now with regard to your finances. Like the "You Are Here" star on maps, knowing your starting point can help you to more efficiently reach your destination. Once you have identified your destination, you can then more efficiently manage the assets that you do have, allowing the money to serve you so that you can embark in a straight line to wherever it is you want to go.

THE TAKE-AWAYS

- Create your Money Map by having an income statement and balance sheet prepared, either by yourself or by a professional.

- A shortsighted view of money is called *microeconomics,* where money is used without considering how it affects the picture of the whole. This view of money always leads to an erosion of finances over the long term.

- To achieve full wealth of all the assets—human, physical, and financial—invest in the big picture, or *macroeconomics.*

- One of the great secrets to building wealth is to live below your means.

- Money by itself is neutral, as are investments and purchases. Ask yourself if the *price* is worth what it will *cost you down the road* with regard to your future goals and objectives.

ACTION STEPS

- Chart your course: Ask yourself where you would like to be ten years from now with regard to your finances. Ask yourself "why" until you get to the bottom, and then write down your answer. Form a concise, one-sentence answer to the question: What is my destination?

- Create your Money Map: Get together all the financial documents you need to get a clear picture of your finances *now*. Create both an income statement and a balance sheet as described earlier in this chapter. You can access a free money map template at BeauHenderson.com or hire someone in your area to help you.

- Design your lifestyle: The first two action exercises will give you both your starting point and your destination. You are now ready to make the trip. Design a budget that you and your family can stick to. Make sure that it follows the principles of macroeconomics by keeping the bigger picture in mind. Get everybody in the household on board so tempting purchases are put into perspective. If time is set aside for relationships and fun experiences, living below your means will not seem like a hardship at all.

- **Bonus Gift**: Download your free copy of the Action Guide for *The RichLife: Ten Investments for True Wealth* at www.RichLifeActionGuide.com.

If you enjoyed this book and want to learn more about the RichLife, go deeper with Beau Henderson's book, *The Richlife: Ten Investments for True Wealth* available here: www.RichLifeBook.com.

About the Author

Beau Henderson is a financial advisor with a philosophy and track record of helping people achieve success with money and life. He is a bestselling author with multiple books including *The Richlife—Ten Investments for True Wealth, 5 Thieves That Will Steal Your Richlife,* and *The New Money Mission.* Beau is also a nationally syndicated radio host and CEO of The Richlife Group. He has been featured in *Forbes, The Wall Street Journal, USA Today, The Huffington Post,* and shares articles, training, and resources for success with life and money at www.BeauHenderson.com.